Wedding Vendor

Handbook

Wedding Vendor

Handbook

Get to the Top and Stay There

Barbara Wallace, CSEP

Master Bridal Consultant TM

Sage House Publishing

Wedding Vendor Handbook
Get to the Top and Stay There
Copyright © 2005, 2006 by Barbara Wallace

Inquiries should be addressed to:

SAGE HOUSE PUBLISHING
PO Box 84
Corona del Mar, California 92625-0084
Phone 949-640-7843

Printed in the United States of America

Cover design by: Zoe Bachelor, Studio Z Mendocino
Edited by: Heather A. Brown

Library of Congress Cataloging-in-Publication Data

Wallace, Barbara
    Wedding Vendor Handbook Get to the Top and Stay There / Wallace, Barbara
    p.201 cm.
    ISBN

Acknowledgements

Writing a book is a community project - whether some of the community knows it or not. The community that contributed to this project is the entire wedding community in which I have worked for eight years as well as my family and friends who have been supportive of me in my career as a wedding planner. The first person to whom I owe thanks is my daughter, Heather Brown, who made me aware of the career of wedding planner in the first place. She called me one day in about 1996 and said "I have the perfect career for you. I read about it in a book of unusual careers." After investigating it and realizing she was right, I jumped into it. It is the perfect career for me and I am fortunate to have had a certain measure of success and much enjoyment while pursuing it. She has continued to give me counsel and I can count on her to be straightforward when I ask her opinion which I value and trust. She also happens to be my editor and web master or, perhaps more accurately, my web mistress. Both have been a huge help to me as well.

Next is Ed Whitehouse, my good friend of many years, who has been quietly supportive of me along the path we've traveled together. There is no way I could do half of what I do without his help - from watering the yard and feeding the cats to just listening to me brainstorm and nodding at the right times.

Then, of course, there is Sharon Jansen of Special Event Business Advisors who was first my friend (years before I ever thought of wedding planning) then became my business coach, and continues to be my friend. She always tells the truth – whether one wants to hear it or not. She's a savvy lady who gave me lots of help and inspiration and continues to do so. I'm honored to be invited repeatedly as a guest speaker to her career planning classes.

Then, there is the myriad of wedding vendors with whom I have worked over the years. Each has taught me something and it is they who have been the inspiration for this book. Some, such as Christopher Aldama, Andy Sarracino and Chris Winn have become my good friends whose special relationships transcend business.

There are also the wedding consultants from all areas of the world whom I have met through the Association of Bridal Consultants. Beginning with Paula Laskelle, whom I met during the first few months I was in business and whom I count as a good friend and colleague, to the many others – both in my local area and from far away - whom I have talked with about the business of weddings so many times.

My business could not run without assistants. I need at least one for every wedding and often more. Wendy Dahl has been the paragon assistant - always professional, cheerful, dependable and just plain adorable. I wish I could clone her. Suzanne Branson and Clara Ross are also wonderful and have been there for me many times, too. They are others I wish I could clone.

And then there are my clients - the lifeblood without whom my career would definitely not exist. I have been fortunate to have some of the best clients on the planet with the vision and taste to put on amazing weddings at all levels. They have been true partnerships resulting in win-wins.

I have also been fortunate to work at some of the most fabulous venues in Southern California and I deeply appreciate the relationships I have with those venues and the ladies and gentlemen there. What a wonderful ride this has been.

Thanks to everyone of you and to anyone else I inadvertently forgot.

Barbara Wallace
Corona del Mar, CA
January 2, 2005

Contents

Part III. Wedding Vendors by Discipline

Note to brides and grooms

While this book is written for wedding vendors, you as a bride or groom might have stumbled across it. You might be surprised at some of the things you read here but it will prepare you to demand the most of your wedding vendors. By asking vendors to live up to your expectations of professionalism based upon what you read here you should have a fabulous wedding and help raise the level of professionalism in the entire wedding industry. Happy wedding!

Introduction

As the planner, producer and director of over 185 weddings, I have had the opportunity to work with a multitude of wedding vendors. They have ranged from the best to the worst. After seeing the wide schism between various vendors and the way they present themselves, I have concluded that there are those who understand how to present themselves properly and those who don't. Many of them, though they are eager to be successful and tap into the multi-billion dollar wedding industry, just don't know how to operate their business any better than they do. But they are hungry for any information that will get them further along the road to the top.

Because I have had a certain measure of success in the wedding field and am open to helping others find their success, many seek and take my advice as to how to improve their business. After dozens of questions from dozens of vendors of all types, I saw the need to write this handbook. It defines what being a "top wedding vendor" means, then tells how any vendor might become and stay a top vendor. It describes what those who "understand" do and shares their methods with established and aspiring wedding vendors alike.

It's a pleasure working with a professional vendor and can be a nightmare working with the opposite. Professionalism does not have anything to do with how much a vendor charges, where they ply their trade or how large a company they are. A one person operation can be more professional than a multi-million dollar company. This book will tell you why.

Because I am a wedding planner and coordinator this book is admittedly coordinator-centric. It's not that I believe the planner or coordinator is better than anyone else on the vendor team, it's that I realize that every good team needs a leader. I liken the job of a wedding coordinator to that of a symphony conductor. Each musician in the symphony is an accomplished player and knows how to do his or her job adequately, perhaps even brilliantly, but the conductor is still at the front leading the orchestra. Each wedding vendor is (or should be) good (or great) at his or her job and the wedding coordinator is simply directing this group. Every group is better with a good leader. Imagine how wonderful it can be with a great leader. Of course, every wedding will not have a coordinator and your bride will likely not be experienced in wedding planning, so when you are on your own on the wedding day it's even more important that you conduct yourself as professionally as possible and be a good team player.

"No one can whistle a symphony. It takes an orchestra to play it." **- H.E. Luccock.**

On the biggest day of most couples' lives there is one goal - to make it the best day possible for the bride and groom. Each vendor must keep that in mind - individually and as a team member. The bridal couple is likely throwing the biggest party they'll ever throw. They are spending a large amount of money. They are emotionally involved. Once they put their trust in us we owe them the best we can give. And it doesn't hurt to make the other team members look good in the process.

As you go through this book you will see anecdotes of experiences that I or another wedding vendor has had in the course of working in the wedding field. Some are so unbelievable that they are funny; others are so unprofessional that they are unbelievable. In either case, they are great examples of what to avoid as you follow your chosen career path to success in the wedding industry.

Remember, it doesn't matter what others are doing or how sloppily they conduct themselves or their business. You must always stay professional. Any one can be mediocre - just a few become outstanding.

You will also see several **"Ironclad Rules"**. These are rules that you must always remember no matter what. **There are no variables to these rules – EVER!**

Best wishes for a quick ascent to the top.

Part I

Definition of the term "Top Wedding Vendor"

What is a top wedding vendor?

A top wedding vendor is one who conducts his or her business professionally during all phases of the wedding process; from the initial contact with the client to the end of their business dealings. This can be months before and after the wedding. It includes professional behavior not only with clients but with fellow vendors and the public in general. As you read through this book you will learn what the term "professional behavior" means and valuable tips on how to practice it daily.

Reputation is your most important asset

The perception people have of you is your reputation. You must always behave in a manner that will establish your reputation as you want it to be, and then continue to behave in such a way that it remains spotless. The more you become known in the wedding industry, the more people will talk about you – that's human nature. It's amazing how vendors talk among themselves, and with clients, and you can gain or lose business based upon that without even knowing it. The best ad campaign in the world will not help if your fellow vendors have reservations about recommending you; if, for example, they have seen you have a tantrum behind the scenes of a setup or if you are known as always being late or sloppy.

It has been said that you are only as good as your last wedding. I would add that any wedding is only as good as its weakest link, meaning that a poor vendor can affect the entire wedding and bring it from wonderful to mundane or even to disaster. You certainly don't ever want to be known as that weakest link.

Be a problem solver

Top wedding vendors are good problem solvers. Being a problem solver rather than a naysayer can be equated with seeing the glass half full rather than half empty. It's looking beyond what you see in front of you into the possibility of doing something another way to get where you need to be. It's thinking beyond the boundaries.

That doesn't mean that everything has to be a new creation or never been done before. It means only that you look at more than one way to do something. It can be as simple as a different placement of the head table in a banquet room, or the way in which food is presented, or the way in which the timeline of the wedding day is planned. It can be a decision you must make instantly on the wedding day due to an unforeseen incident either small or very large. It's the ability to think on your feet and come up with at least an adequate solution if not a perfect one.

Another coordinator told a story of a wedding where the florist didn't show up and couldn't be reached. Saying it was too late to do anything, the coordinator believed she could only "grieve" with the bride about the lack of flowers. This was a disservice to the bride. With a little creativity, and a few minutes delay of the wedding, the coordinator could have gone into problem solving mode and either sent the groomsmen to the supermarket to buy all the flowers they could find or to the side of the road to pick whatever greens or flowers they could to at least make a bridal bouquet and a boutonniere which the coordinator would have tied with the ribbon she should be carrying in her emergency kit.

Some people are better problem solvers than others. Some don't solve problems due to a lack of creativity, others out of laziness, boredom or overwork. Of course, it's easier to take the known path, but I would encourage you to always keep pushing yourself to look with new eyes, think with an open mind and feel with a full heart.

It also helps to keep your sense of humor during the challenging periods of your job. I don't mean acting like a comic or clowning. I mean keeping a feeling of lightness to balance out the stress that is inevitable. While you must take your job and the results you wish to achieve seriously, its best not to take *yourself* too seriously. You must also develop the insight of when to accept things you cannot change. Move on when you have done all you can to try to right the wrong and nothing more can change.

A wedding is show business

All wedding vendors are in show business. It's as simple as that. Planning and executing a wedding is not unlike a theatrical production. Albeit, a theatre production with only one performance. We vendors only get one time to get it right. There are no dress rehearsals or second chances. That's why it is most important that we do an exemplary job and give the bride and groom our very best on their wedding day.

Ironclad Rule # 1: **Behind-the-scenes things should never be seen by the guests.**

This means all set up must be done before the guests walk in and all break down done after they leave. There should be a mystique surrounding the wedding and reception (or any event for that matter) that gives the impression it's happening effortlessly, even if things are a shambles behind the scenes. The guests must never know about any of your problems or difficulties in carrying out your job. You must strive to always carry yourself confidently and have a positive expression on your face whenever you are in sight of any guests. Never run or appear harried or they will read your mood and body language and immediately assume (even incorrectly) that something is wrong. That perception can travel like wildfire through the group and change the tone of the event.

This is a service industry

It's important to remember that as a wedding vendor you are in a service industry. Part of being in service is to interact pleasantly with everyone with whom you come in contact. If you are unwilling or unable to be pleasant, even when you are crabby on the inside, you must evaluate whether this is the best industry for you.

A wedding should be one of the happiest days of a bride and groom's lives. It will most likely not be a perfect day simply because "perfect" is hard to come by anywhere, plus the concept of perfection is very subjective. In fact, I make it a habit to never use the word "perfect" when I describe how a wedding will be. But that does not mean I don't strive for perfection and give the best possible service at all times. It just means that it's best not to set up expectations that are subjective.

I impress upon my assistants to never leave paperwork such as the wedding day timeline (our gospel for the day) where guests will see it. I concluded this when a friend attended a wedding in which I had no involvement. He mentioned that the reception had run late by over an hour the whole time. How did he know that? He had seen a copy of the timeline lying around and read it. There went part of the mystique. Probably several of the other guests were told of this discovery contributing further to the disappearance of the precious mystique.

Stay Current

Though bound by traditions that might be either cultural or religious, wedding styles do change over the years. Some brides want to put a spin on those traditions to make their wedding unique - often in small ways. Even if they don't want to tinker with the traditions they might want unique décor, which can be as simple as the fold of the napkin or as elaborate as transforming the reception to a Moroccan palace. Popular bridal and gossip magazines are constantly coming up with new ideas and looks (they want to sell magazines, after all) and your brides will read them voraciously. It behooves you to be aware of them as well.

You'll be surprised at how many times you'll be shown pictures from magazines or wedding books that are "exactly" what the bride wants. Other times they'll be an inspiration that can be a springboard to your new ideas. While you don't want to copy others, you'll see trends emerge. Even if you're a vendor who isn't involved in the design process you'll need to stay current as styles of videography and photography, for example, change just as rapidly as design elements do.

By staying current you'll be able to spot trends as they appear and offer your brides and grooms the up to the minute information they desire. You owe it to them to know the latest trends in your field, whether it be a new kind of film or camera, new styles of shooting video or photography, new looks in décor, flowers or gowns, ad infinitum.

Besides magazines and books, networking with your peers at trade organizations and conferences is invaluable. You'll be introduced to new products, new ideas and new people and find that time spent there energizes you. Offer to participate by presenting a seminar and you'll find that you'll get even more out of it. Most disciplines have their own trade organization that meets nationally once per year and locally more frequently. See the Appendix for a list of such groups. Inquire of your peers if there is a pertinent group in your area or start one if there isn't.

Working with high-end clients

It seems that all vendors want high end clients as there is a perception that they spend more freely and have unlimited funds. In some cases that is true but certainly not always. Often high-end clients are far more demanding than average and expect more service and value for their money.

They are used to getting what they want in both their business and personal lives and expect you to deliver it, especially when they are paying a premium price. Just charging a high price does not put you in the league to work with high end clients. You must also have the business experience and social savvy to play on that field or you could find yourself in over your head, getting a bad reputation or, in the worst case, even being sued.

Tailoring your business to the upper echelon is fine but be sure you carefully work your way up to that level so each step you take is on a solid foundation. Garner your great reputation with baby steps and soon you'll be able to take huge strides. This doesn't necessarily mean you have to progress slowly. It just means you should progress carefully.

How long will it take to get to the top?

The question of how long it will take to become a top wedding vendor is different in every case. Both your experience in business and in life will affect it because, if you have more of either (or both) it could streamline the process for you. You will, of course, encounter more challenges in starting your business at square one with no network or customer base, and perhaps no experience in the special event industry, than someone with some know-how in their field of pursuit. As a general rule, it seems that you should expect to take about 3 to 4 years for your business to come into its own. By that I mean that you've hit your stride and have become known in your field. You will have developed a good network for referrals and become very confident in your product or service and have the business part of it running smoothly and efficiently. Your income should have increased to a decent level.

This is not to say that you will have neither success nor good income until that time, but there is an inevitable curve that a new business must climb. It's a process and a little like climbing a mountain. Some climbers can practically run up a mountainside while others must take it step by step. But with perseverance they all can reach the top. Some start out in better shape that others so might get there faster just as having some experience will help you get a new business off the ground more quickly. By focusing on your goals and consistently practicing the information you are about to read, your climb to the top should be easier and faster than most.

Part Two

Elements of Being a Top Wedding Vendor

Professionalism

Professionalism is the most important element of being a top wedding vendor and it is a huge one. It encompasses everything from your appearance, behavior and manners during the selling and servicing phases with your clients to day to day interaction with your colleagues and other wedding vendors in all of your business dealings. It is your persona. It is what your reputation in the wedding industry will be based upon and must be practiced at all times.

Following is a discussion of the various elements that make up the concept of professionalism. You probably already practice many of them but honing those and adding others can serve to boost you to a higher level in your chosen career.

Appearance/dress

Your clothing and appearance are fully in your control and should be given special attention since they contribute greatly to the first impression your prospective clients and others will get. Only your telephone skills will precede you. (A discussion on that topic follows.)

Remember that you have just one time to make a first impression, whether it is in person or by telephone, so make it the best you can.

Dress as you want to be perceived

Always dress as you want people to perceive you. That's a simple rule to keep in mind as you take a last look in the mirror before leaving for a business meeting or the wedding. Ask yourself, "Does how I look today fit the image I wish to convey to those I'm meeting?" If it doesn't, change into something that does and go to the meeting with confidence.

If you want to show them you are in charge and a no-nonsense person, a well tailored, conservative business suit in a dark color will indicate that. Should you want to convey your creativity you can add some dashes with a bold tie or scarf, a unique piece of jewelry or an unusual color combination, but you don't have to wear the latest fads or dress like a Bohemian artist to show your creativity.

For meetings it's a good idea to dress as your clients do but I would suggest that you dress more up than down. For example, if you are meeting a client in her office and it is known to be a casual company, my advice would be to dress up slightly more than you expect her to be. If you are meeting a client in her home on a weekend she will most likely be dressed casually, but it is important that you keep your professional edge by appearing in business attire –after all you are at work. You must use your best judgment, of course, but keep in mind this quote from business writer and columnist, Harvey McKay: "There are no casual days when trying to win a client". You don't want your prospective clients to be turned off by your being overly formal, of course, but there seems to be little danger in that in today's world.

Wear attire appropriate to your field. A baker, for example, would not be expected to appear in a three piece business suit but certainly a clean apron over fresh checked pants and a spotless baker's smock would be appropriate. Even if you normally wear jeans in your shop avoid them for interviews and sales meetings. Jeans are not appropriate business attire unless you are a cowboy.

Grooming and hygiene are of utmost importance, especially when you are aiming to work in the realm of high-end weddings where such clients are used to being surrounded by the best. Your clothing must be clean and pressed and worn neatly. Untucked shirttails or too long pants look sloppy, as do long or flowing dresses and multiple layers of oversized clothing. If you are overweight keep in mind that looser clothing doesn't necessarily hide your excess weight. It can make you look larger, so special attention should be given to your choice of clothing. Excessive or flashy jewelry should be avoided by both men and women and fragrance should be used sparingly. Food servers/preparers should never wear fragrance. Faddish or heavy makeup for women is inappropriate in business. It goes without saying that there should be no gum chewing.

Keep your nails well manicured (chipped polish is a big turn-off) and your hair clean and in an attractive and appropriate color and style for your job and age. Pay special attention to the length of your hair. Don't wear it too long. Most women over about 30 don't look good with hair longer than shoulder length and flowing hair isn't very professional. If you insist on wearing your hair long tie it back neatly during your working hours. Men with long hair should look at themselves with a critical eye to make sure they don't look dated or sloppy.

Keep your shoes shined and in good repair and wear the appropriate style for the job you will be performing. Spike heels for women become very uncomfortable in a short time, and open toes should be avoided. Tennis shoes are not appropriate except for behind the scenes set up. Many vendors, especially women, carry a change of shoes on the wedding day knowing that eight to ten hours on their feet will feel like twice as long in the same pair of shoes.

Here's a trick I use when I have a weekend with back to back weddings. I plunge my feet into ice water for a few minutes when I return from the first gig and again as I'm getting ready on the second day. I also take an ibuprofen tablet before, during and after each wedding as I find that controls the swelling which causes much of the discomfort.

Have different wardrobes for your business and social lives, and keep the line between them well-drawn. You might be a mambo queen during your free time, but that attire would not be appropriate for regular wedding business. An interesting concept I once heard was that your credibility in business correlates directly with the amount of skin you have showing at work – think of the contrast between a nun and a stripper. Especially if you are a woman, keep that in mind as you choose your business wardrobe. Low necklines, short skirts and tight clothes are not the mark of a professional in most lines of work.

On the wedding day choose an outfit that blends in with what the guests will be wearing. This means dressing in keeping with the formality of the wedding, although sleeveless is never appropriate unless it is part of a band costume. For a black tie wedding, a photographer or videographer, for instance, should not wear khakis or just a sport coat. Vendors can safely be attired in all black at almost all weddings and I think that looks best. However, be sure to select appropriate styles as discussed above – not just a black T-shirt and jeans. It's best to avoid bright or strong colors, and please, no one should wear white except

> One wedding vendor I encountered was a non-performing member of a band that was hired by the bride before I was hired. She wore a bright aqua sweater and could be seen prominently throughout the finished wedding video officiously walking back and forth across the dance floor and around the room during the evening. She was like a beacon in the sea of black evening wear, and her constant film presence became a challenge to the videographer during the editing process.

for the bride. As a vendor you should blend into the background, not be a focal point.

Protocol/dress code

I expect all those who assist me at a wedding or at other business functions to dress and behave in a professional manner, and that includes interns or high-school students that I might be mentoring. I have a printed guideline of what I expect of them. Assistants, interns or those I'm mentoring are an extension of my business and must represent themselves as such. Please see the appendix for a copy of my protocol.

Your vehicle

The vehicle you drive says something about you and no matter what brand or style, it should be kept clean and free of clutter. Naturally there should be no dents, torn seats or spots on the carpet. If you are trying to sell yourself as an organized, efficient and talented wedding vendor your vehicle can reinforce that – or conversely, work against your image.

Choose a make and model that conveys the image you want to project. You want to look prosperous and successful without looking pretentious. One photographer I know says he has chosen his car brand (Audi) to be just about where, but not more than, his client's cars are (often BMW or similar) as he wants to look prosperous but not extravagant. He says that he has many brides unexpectedly ride in his car on their wedding day to make a quick dash to the beach or off the premises to get a few unusual shots and he's always sure to keep his car clean and neat because of that. Why not keep the car clean and neat for yourself as well? You deserve that, too.

If you occasionally need a truck or van in your type of business, you might find it just as reasonable to rent one as needed rather then investing in the purchase of such a vehicle. That way you can get exactly the capacity needed for each job without the expense of maintaining it on a daily basis.

Ironclad Rule #2: **You MUST let others with whom you are working know where things stand and how they are progressing.**

Follow up...

One of the most important elements of professionalism is follow up. It absolutely must be employed in every step and for every relationship in the business of planning a wedding.

... With clients

The first contact from a client might be a phone message of inquiry. Ideally, you should be in your office and answer the telephone on the second or third ring but, realistically, many wedding vendors are solo proprietors and aren't at their phone every minute. Get back to that prospective client by the next day at the very latest- in the first few hours after the call if at all possible. That very gesture will show them that you are professional and available for them which will extrapolate into continued good service. See a more complete discussion of telephone etiquette in the section entitled "Telephones".

For established clients, you must keep them apprised of what's going on with their wedding planning. It's always best to contact them before they contact you especially if you owe them an answer or there is a pivotal point that will affect other phases of the planning process or other vendors. An example is that they are waiting to print the program until you get back to them with the composer of a song that will be listed therein. Even if you cannot find the needed information in a timely manner, call them to let them know you are working on it and when they can expect to hear from you.

In these days of e-mail it's easy to keep clients and vendors alike informed of every detail plus, you can have a printed record to refresh your memory or confirm that you have done something.

... With other vendors

Other vendors must be treated with the same respect as a client. The way you treat them becomes part of your reputation and your business persona. Besides keeping them informed of what's going on with the particular wedding you're mutually involved in, it builds a relationship between the two of you and – guess what - another vendor becomes a great referral source for you.

Many fellow vendors have complimented me for being on top of things after I've made a simple phone call or sent an e-mail to them to verify something or to advise them of even a minor point that I thought they should know. Several have even told me I was the first wedding coordinator who had ever called them in advance of a wedding, which is a huge shock to me. It makes me wonder what other wedding coordinators are doing.

After wedding...

When the wedding is over the client and other vendors don't just disappear off the face of the earth. It's important to debrief and learn how you can improve your performance next time. You must continually be on the lookout for areas of improvement. Since there has never been the perfect wedding (and probably never will be) we all should learn something from every wedding. Once we get complacent or too cocky we lose our edge and then we lose our reputation.

...with clients

Because brides and grooms usually depart for their honeymoon immediately after the wedding it's often difficult to reach them by telephone. In my business, I use a hand written note of thanks for my final contact with them. Included is a two-sided single page evaluation sheet called "Service Questionnaire" (see the appendix for a copy of that form) in which I ask them to rate, among other things, the quality of service I have provided to them and the quality of the vendors I have referred. This feedback is invaluable and also provides some great quotes for use as testimonials on my website or in my portfolio. By the way, such quotes should never give the full name of the clients without their written permission. I use only their initials to protect my clients' privacy.

Follow up with a telephone call or meeting after they return from their trip if there are points that need discussion.

... with other vendors

Vendors with whom you often work should be telephoned after the wedding to thank them for their work or to discuss things that could be better next time. If they have gone above and beyond, a written note, which they can include in their portfolio, should be sent. You will find that they often include such a letter or note in their portfolio and it becomes another bit of advertisement for you as brides see your name all over town.

New vendors or those with whom you are working for the first time with whom you want to build a relationship can be sent a written note of thanks. However, a phone call and a chat will be a more personal connection and give you valuable time together.

A good mantra to recite: *"I can never write too many thank you notes."*

Behavior, manners and etiquette

A hot topic! Behavior, manners and etiquette contribute to that first impression that you can't change. It's who you are to the world and, as mentioned above, becomes part of your persona and image.

Sales phase

The initial contact with your client will most often be by telephone or often now through your website. This is the time you'll have to make that invaluable "first impression". Make it representative of who you are and what your business is so you can attract the kind of client you want. Have a well thought out and practiced sales pitch that will show a prospective client just what you will provide for them for the price you charge. For more on this see the section entitled Marketing, Sales, Advertising and Publicity.

Be punctual

This is a forgone conclusion. When you book the appointment get the exact address and directions to it. Then check them on a street map if you don't know the area. Take the client's cell phone number and give them yours so if anything happens, such as an unexpected traffic jam, you can be in immediate contact. If you are meeting them in a public place arrange the exact location you will meet them to avoid each of you waiting at a different entrance, which has happened more than once.

Ironclad Rule #3:
Don't bash the competition.

Don't bash the competition

A client and I once met with a talented new florist who took an undue amount of time to send a proposal and failed to return my calls asking when it would be ready. After several attempts and no results I finally called the florist and told him not to bother even sending it as we needed to move ahead and his lack of response was holding up our decision making. He then called the client directly with a tirade saying he was the best and she was making a mistake by not hiring him and so forth. He came off as very unprofessional and slightly unstable and further cemented in our minds why he wouldn't make a good member of our team. I have never referred him since and never will.

During most meetings you'll hear other vendor names mentioned. Many will be in other disciplines and it's perfectly OK to volunteer a good recommendation about them if you have worked with them and know their quality. Cream rises to the top and good vendors stand out. Chances are the client will hear the same thing from others they are talking to. If you are asked for an opinion you may cautiously state *your* experience with that vendor even if it is not a good one- as long as you don't turn your opinion into a rip session and as long as you have *personal* experience. Hearsay is not acceptable here.

It's <u>NEVER</u> OK to bash a vendor in your own discipline, especially if you perceive them as your direct competition and want the job for which you are being interviewed. It will often work in the opposite direction and just make you look bad. Your duty is to let the prospective client know by your great credentials and positive sales pitch how you can give them what they want without resorting to negative comments, either spoken or physical (e.g. eye rolling, head shaking or hand waving) about others.

If you don't get the job, it's usually best. You certainly don't want a client who isn't comfortable with you. If you are consistently losing jobs you should examine your sales presentation as described in the Marketing section below.

Don't go direct to a client without permission if a planner has brought them to you

Wedding planners and coordinators work in different ways. Some mark up vendor services to the client by asking you to bill their company. Their company pays your bill and then bills a higher amount to the client. This amount becomes their profit margin. Most do not do this, preferring to have you and the client contract directly. However, during the pre-contract phase you should respect the planner's relationship with their client and not go behind the planner's back to contact that client directly.

After you are contracted, make sure the planner agrees that you may contact the client directly and, if you do, always copy the planner on any written material you send, including a copy of the signed contract, and keep her apprised by telephone or e-mail of any discussions you and the client have, especially those involving material changes that will affect the wedding day. The most professional vendors I know are those that ask permission to give my client even a business card saying "we are your company when we work with your client." Most of the time I don't mind them giving their card but sometimes prefer that all communication goes through me, so I very much appreciate their awareness of this.

Respect the Wedding Coordinator's Referral List

When clients hire a wedding coordinator they often do so because of the vendors they will refer. Most coordinators have a list of vendors they have worked with repeatedly, whom they know and trust. They assemble the team for the client based on the client's needs, taste and budget.

As a vendor you might have other vendors you know and like and want to work with. However, it is not your place to refer them to a client that was referred to you by a wedding coordinator. Your preference might be someone unknown to the coordinator or someone known to the coordinator but not preferred by her. You are treading on thin ice when you start usurping the coordinator's job and risk not being referred by her in the future. Think of how it would be if the tables were turned. For example, if you are a photographer would you like it if she told your client what lab to use to process your photos?

Planning Phase

This is the long term part of the relationship. It will usually be many months and it will include times when you're frightfully busy as well as when you're slow. We can't choose the times our clients will call us so must be ready for anything whenever the phone rings. No matter what, get back to your client or fellow vendor as soon as you possibly can. That means within one day of their contacting you, if even to say "I'm in an event this weekend and will talk to you in depth Monday" or "I've contacted the vendor you've asked about and will contact you as soon as I get the information back from him."

Ironclad Rule #4: NEVER answer your phone when you are not prepared to talk intelligently.

It's far better to get the message on your voice mail than to tell a caller that you're running out the door and can't talk now, or to interrupt someone you are already conversing with and tell the new caller you can't talk now, or that you're in traffic and can't talk, or whatever it is. It's an insult to both the caller on the line and the new caller to be treated that way and is an inefficient way to do business. It's also an insult to someone with whom you are meeting to answer a call during that meeting. You are indicating that you have no respect for their time or the subject about which you are meeting and that something or someone else is more important. One exception is, if you are expecting a call that has to do with the subject of the meeting for which you need an immediate answer and you have advised the person with whom you are meeting that you will take the call. Get Caller ID on your phone so you can screen the call and answer only if you know it's coming from the person you must talk to. If necessary, leave the room or go to a more private area to conduct your business without disturbing others.

I always wonder why people feel compelled to answer the phone anytime it rings, no matter where they are or what they are doing. Remember your telephone is for your convenience - not necessarily the caller's.

Before answering any call train yourself to think, "If this is a first call from a prospective client do I have the time and mindset to talk to them at the moment and give my sales pitch to them?" If not, don't answer it. It can be difficult at first, to stand by the phone and let it ring, but once you learn how, it becomes easy. If yours is a mobile phone please turn it off when you're at the bank and in other public places. Others around you are not interested in hearing you conduct your business loudly or worse yet chatting on aimlessly about seemingly inconsequential things. You come off as a buffoon rather than a tycoon as much as you might think it makes you look important. Be aware that others around you are all potential clients or referrals, and you never know who is overhearing you.

Treat your clients and other vendors as you would like to be treated by them (hmm-doesn't this sound like the old Golden Rule?). This means following up promptly, keeping them informed, getting their contracts and other paperwork back to them promptly, giving them clear instructions as to what will be expected of them on the wedding day, and generally being a good team member.

Wedding Day

The wedding day is the culmination of the many hours of planning and preparation. It's the <u>only</u> time we have to get it right and it must be as near to perfect as we can humanly make it. This is no time to drop the ball so everything must be checked and rechecked in advance to ensure that nothing will fall between the cracks.

Set up

I once coordinated a wedding at a five star resort in southern California where I had "inherited" the florist – the mom had hired them before she hired me. They are a well known company and were doing extensive décor for the ceremony. Imagine my horror when I saw one of the decorators working with his shirt off in a very public area of the hotel. Not only was it inappropriate and un-professional but he didn't even have a nice body to look at. On top of all that, they were very late in finishing their set up which delayed the entire pre-ceremony photos that the bride and groom wanted.

This is usually a high tension time as all vendors are cramming in to the same space trying to do their job in what often is a condensed period of time. There is nothing as nice as working with civilized people who create a calm and professional atmosphere. Emotions often are high, especially during the set up of a complicated event when literally dozens of vendors and their crews are vying for the same loading dock, door or floor space, and it is important that all remain calm and cool.

Because we are all part of the team hired to make this event come off as perfectly as possible, we are all responsible for the result and are therefore responsible for pulling our own weight and picking up the slack when a fellow vendor is having problems with their portion.

Naturally you must take care of your own part first but being considerate of those around you makes a very favorable impression and goes a long way toward building your reputation as a professional.

Treat other vendors politely, especially in front of the guests and wedding party that may have wandered in to the set-up area. Ideally, of course, no one but vendors will see this phase, but sometimes others peek in out of curiosity and must be treated politely even if being asked to leave.

Always dress professionally during set up, especially where guests or other patrons of the venue can see you. A set up crew should be in matching T- or polo shirts, all black or some other appropriate attire for the job. It is said that the show begins at the curb, so from the time your truck drives up you are on-stage and must act accordingly. I might add that the show ends at that same curb, so carry that professional demeanor all the way through tear down even if it is 2:00 AM and you've been up for 20 hours.

An interesting alcohol related incident is kind of a wakeup call relative to the issue of the appearance of impropriety was told to me by a wedding coordinator. The mother of the bride asked him to get her a drink during the photo session. He graciously went to the bar and got the drink which he took to the mom. However, after the wedding the bride asked him why he had been drinking on the wedding day saying that a bridesmaid had seen him go to the bar and get a drink. It appeared that he had obtained it for himself and it took some explaining to make the bride realize the truth. To avoid such an issue it would have been prudent to ask a server to deliver the drink to the mom or at least the coordinator could have carried it to her on a tray.

Ironclad Rule #5: **Do not curse or have tantrums**.

Enough said.

Parking on the wedding day

Be very careful where you park your vehicle, especially after you have finished unloading your gear. Loading docks are notoriously inadequate and there are often a large number of vehicles of all sizes vying for the same docking space, particularly when the facility is hosting multiple events on the same day. Keep in mind that the regular deliveries of a hotel come thorough that loading dock and their purchasing department is far more interested in that than they are your flowers or music equipment for this single event.

To assume that an empty space is saved for your car is jumping to a conclusion that often creates problems for other deliveries. Don't be one of those vendors who thinks he is special, that everyone else but him has to follow the rules and that he can conveniently park right in front. For a newly arriving vendor to have to run around during the busiest time of the set up and find out whose car is blocking the way is not only annoying but also selfish and shows a lack of concern for the team.

Some venues will actually tow a car that has been left unattended or in the way at the loading dock. Imagine coming out at midnight ready to go home after a hard gig and discovering your car missing.

Eating and drinking at reception

Keep foremost in your mind that you are NOT a guest at this wedding. No matter what kind of rapport you have developed with your client, you are not a guest. You are hired and you are working and must be on duty at all times. Even if you are doing the job as a favor to the bride and groom free of charge you should perform as a professional.

At one wedding I coordinated the photographer had already been hired and I was working with him for the first time on the wedding day. As he was taking the post-ceremony photos the hotel staff brought out a cart of champagne and hors d'oeuvres for the wedding party. Imagine my horror when the photographer began to help himself to the food and was talking with his mouth full giving directions as to how they should pose. He stopped that behavior once I drew him aside and explained that the food was for the guests not the vendors, but as a professional that was something he should have known with out an impromptu etiquette lesson.

Ironclad Rule #6: **Under NO circumstances are you to drink any alcoholic beverages at an event.**

This is so important that I am going to say it again. - this time in all capital letters. UNDER NO CIRCUMSTANCES ARE YOU TO DRINK ANY ALCOHOLIC BEVERAGES AT AN EVENT.

If it isn't obvious why, let me give you several cogent reasons:

A band I inherited as the coordinator of one wedding insisted through their contract with the client that they have a hot meal served to them because "they work so hard". The usual vendor fare at this hotel was a sandwich buffet served to allow vendors to quickly grab their meal while taking a fifteen to twenty minute break. In this case the client had to pay for a full meal for the band members who expected a half hour break for their meal. The other alternative written into their contract was that they would order room service if such a meal was not served to them. This was not a name band with a demanding rider, but just a local band with an inflated ego. I found their demands prima donna-like. After all, all of the vendors work hard on the wedding day and many I have worked with are so conscientious they don't even plan to take a meal break during the time. The upshot of this band's "working so hard" is that they had roadies to set up and break down and didn't even work as long as the photographer at that event who, by the way, was grateful to get a few minutes to sit and enjoy the sandwich buffet.

1.   No one should drink on the job. I'm sure you as a customer or client do not want your bank teller, surgeon, plumber, gas station attendant, teacher (continue to fill in the blanks here) drinking while they are serving you, so why would any client want you to be drinking when you are serving them?

2.   You are not a guest at this event and the alcohol is not provided for your pleasure. It is for the guests and you are hired help for this event. The bar tab can be a large expense and some brides and grooms must watch their budget closely, so adding to the bar tab is a strain for them even if it isn't also inappropriate.

3.   It appears unprofessional (which it is). A good rule to adopt for yourself and those employed by you is not to drink anything alcoholic on the premises where you are working – even after the gig. It is important to avoid any suggestion of impropriety and stay above reproach at all times.

Band members and musicians tend to be especially lax on this rule. Maybe it's because many have a club background and that is often tolerated in that atmosphere. It is very important that they understand the importance of this strict rule and abide by it to the letter. I will not refer a band again if I have seen their members drinking.

I would suggest that it's best not to even approach the bar as it may look like you are acting as a guest and/or are taking an alcoholic beverage. Ask a server to get you a glass of water or a soda and drink it discreetly.

Ironclad Rule #7: You are NOT to eat any of the hors d'oeuvres that are being passed for the guests - even if you are starving.

As an adult and a professional it's your responsibility to take care of eating before you come to the event.

It's customary, though not mandatory, to provide a meal for any vendors working over about 4 hours on the wedding day. It is your responsibility to check in advance (usually through the coordinator) that this is being offered. Otherwise, bring your own snack and discreetly have it on a break. Any food you are invited to consume should be eaten out of sight of the guests on a conveniently scheduled break. Don't expect gourmet food- often a box lunch or sandwich is the vendor fare but occasionally there is an overage of food from the guests' meal and the banquet captain will offer it to the vendors. Sometimes the vendors are invited to go through the buffet line after all the guests have eaten. Whatever the arrangement, do it politely and discreetly.

A photographer I was working with for the first time at one wedding jumped into the buffet line right after bride and groom. I was shocked to see that and asked him what he was doing. He said he had to eat at the exact time they did or he might miss some photos which is absolutely ridiculous. The caterer had previously explained that she had paper plates for the vendors and that all would be welcome to go through the buffet line after all guests had been served. She happened to come by the buffet just as this photographer was helping himself and reiterated her arrangement and politely asked him to step aside so the parents of the couple could get their meal. He began loudly berating her saying he had never been treated so badly and that he would be sure to never refer her and generally acting obnoxious.

Occasionally a couple will invite the vendors to dine with the guests. Discourage this for several reasons:

1. We vendors are hired help that day (I don't care if you are a rocket scientist that moonlights doing wedding videos, you are still a hired hand that day and should act as such). Reasoning- people don't ask their maids to sit at the dining table with them as they entertain so why should the vendors expect to dine with the guests.

2. Wedding guests feel slighted if they are the ones who have to sit at a table with the vendors. They never know if they have to converse with the vendors or ignore them.

3. Vendor meals are usually less costly than the guests' food and your client needn't incur the extra expense of serving the higher priced food to you.

4. Vendor meals are best being one course meals that can be eaten quickly so we are not away from the reception for protracted periods.

If you are invited to go through the buffet line, do it only after all guests have been through the line, and be discreet. Take your reasonably filled plate to an out of sight corner or back room to eat and remove it when you are finished. The better venues will set a separate table in a nearby room for the vendors and have a server get beverages and bus but if not, you'll have to use your judgment to be as unobtrusive as possible.

Interacting with guests and other vendors during the event

Once again, you are NOT a guest at this event. You are not to mingle with the guests and join their private conversations. Speak politely when they address you and offer to assist them when necessary, or direct them to someone who can assist them. Be pleasant and helpful but maintain a professional distance. Do not flirt with or come on to attractive attendees. This is a job, not a pick up opportunity. You must never join the festivities and dance unless you are specifically hired for that purpose.

If your crew must move things, such as florals from the ceremony to the reception, and they will be seen by guests, always have them in professional attire (all black is always appropriate). Make sure they know in advance the least intrusive route and that they should carry out their project as discreetly as possible. It's your responsibility to make this transition smooth and unobtrusive.

If you are providing some kind of onsite assistance, such as a lighting operator, make sure he or she is appropriately attired (here again all black works well), and that the job is carried out discreetly.

Handing out your business cards

Occasionally a guest or someone else will ask you for a business card as you perform your duties at a wedding. The truly professional vendor realizes that he is a member of a team and, if he was brought to that team by the wedding planner or coordinator, he will not pass his business card out without direct permission from the planner or will hand the planner's card out or refer that person directly to the planner. Make sure you and the planner who referred you have discussed this issue in advance so you both know what is expected. Some planners handle payment of all phases of the wedding and all vendors appear to the client to be part of that planner's company. In that case they would likely even be wearing the planner's logo on their clothing at set up and strike.

Thanking others for referrals

Once you are established as a top wedding vendor you will find that more and more of your business comes from referrals by others. It can be from former clients (that's why it's important to do an outstanding job every time) or from other vendors, which is why you should <u>always</u> carry out your job in an extremely professional way. You are "on stage" at every wedding and other vendors are seeing your every move. If you do an incredible job they notice, believe me.

Every time a prospective client calls to inquire about your services, if they don't volunteer the information, you should ask how they heard about you and make a note of it. Then call, e-mail or write a note of thanks to the referring party right away, even if you are not hired. A simple follow up thank you is so appreciated (think how much you enjoy receiving one). It let's them know that their referral was followed up on by the client plus it lets them know you appreciate their giving your name to others. Remember the mantra: ***"I can never write too many thank you notes."***

If you find that you are getting referrals over and over from the same vendor, you can send a gift, the value of which should be commensurate with the amount of business they have sent you. It can be something at the holidays or something every few months, or both, or even something every time you get a job from a referral they gave. You will have to decide what is appropriate. You neither want to appear too cheap nor too extravagant so take an educated guess from what you've seen in your local area or ask other vendors what they do. Some ideas are taking them to lunch periodically, sending a box of candy, cookies, a food basket or other treats for their whole office to enjoy, giving a gift certificate to a nice restaurant or a store you know they like or a gift certificate to a spa for a massage or facial, or even sending a check which is always an appreciated gift.

Remember this is marketing money you are spending. Every referral you get from another wedding professional is advertising you did not have to do through another source. You are essentially getting pre-qualified clients and will find that many fellow vendors will give you a wonderful recommendation based on how they've seen you work and your continuing good reputation. This should be worth a lot to you.

Thanking clients for business

This is an issue that has several opinions attached to it. It's always appropriate to write a thank you note to your bride and groom when the event is over - remember the mantra. They, after all, entrusted their most important day to you and your expertise. Whether to give them a gift is less clear. Some wedding vendors give every client a gift, some give a gift only those clients who have hired them for their largest service package (if that's how your pricing structure is set up) and some give no gift at all. You must determine what is right for you, your clients and both the discipline and geographical area in which you work.

If you elect to give a gift make sure the value is appropriate to the service you have provided. Giving a $150 Tiffany silver picture frame, for example, might not be appropriate for a wedding for which you performed minimal services but would be fine for one in which you provided months of personal assistance. Some wedding vendors actually build the cost of a gift into their fee and plan to spend about 5% of the fee for the gift. A couple of examples: for a $6000 fee you'd give a $300 gift and for a $2500 fee you'd give a $125 gift.

Generally, I don't believe a client expects a gift from a vendor and will often give the vendor a gift in the way of a tip – especially in a service profession that has no tangible product involved. If you are in a business that provides a product, such as a photographer, you could certainly upgrade or throw in something free to the clients and explain that it's a wedding gift from you.

Team play

This section could well be the first in this book as it's such an important part of being a top wedding vendor. There is a common goal for all wedding vendors associated with the same wedding and that's to make the bride and groom's day wonderful. We all work together to that end and my belief is that it doesn't hurt to make each other look good in the process.

We have to do everything we can to make the day turn out well, and if that means helping each other during a particularly tight room turn or assisting a fellow vendor getting into a crowded loading dock that's what must be done. This doesn't mean slacking and expecting other vendors to pick up your slack. It also doesn't mean not bringing enough of your own crew and expecting another vendor to help you. These are not the modus operandi of a top wedding vendor, but helping another who's in an unavoidable or unexpected jam is.

An excellent example is that the photographer and videographer must work as a team, even if they are meeting for the very first time on the wedding day. One of the worst things they can do is to place themselves so they are constantly in each other's shots. This also holds true for the coordinator and other vendors who also should be aware of where they are in relation to the photos being taken.

Confidentiality

It is incumbent upon you as a high end wedding vendor to keep your client's information strictly confidential. That might include even their name but certainly the amount of their budget and their personal information. If you get called upon to speak to the press about the wedding of a high profile client you must be discreet in discussing it and should do so only if they have given you permission to even acknowledge that the wedding took place. Remember, the press is looking for things out of the ordinary as that's what makes interesting stories. So weddings with eye-popping budgets are interesting to readers but could be an embarrassment to your clients.

It's imperative that you have some kind of a signed form that indicates how much if anything you may divulge about a client, whether high profile or not. It should be signed at the time your contract is signed and can be a paragraph in the contract itself or an additional page. Discuss with your legal advisor how best to incorporate it.

Examples of what to consider are: May you list them as a client? May you use a quote from them in your testimonials? If so, may you use their full name or only initials? How about the city where they live, may you list that? May you use them as a reference? May you give their telephone number to a prospective client to call for a reference? May you have photos in your portfolio of their wedding? May you include their likeness as well? If showing the face of your client or any of their guests on your advertising or marketing material, you might have to have a model release so be sure to investigate this issue before using such photos.

Conducting Business

Your in-office procedures and the way you conduct your business greatly contribute to your becoming and staying a top wedding vendor, as they are another way for your professionalism to shine through. It's important to establish them early in your business and continually refine them as you become more adept in your field. Some vendors consider the following too dry - the un-fun part of their job - and tend to ignore it. Perhaps that's for a lack of understanding. However, there are professionals to assist you in all phases of establishing and running your business and you will find your business easier to manage with all this in place.

One sign of a professional is to know when to get help for your business and using the excuse "I'm a new (or small) business and can't afford it" is just not acceptable.

Contract

Many business owners, especially new small business owners, are petrified at the mention of the word "contract", thinking it has to be a long document full of legalese. It's nothing to be afraid of. A contract is merely a written and signed document setting out the terms which will govern the agreement for goods and/or services between you and your client or customer.

Ironclad Rule #8: **Have a contract – and make it a good one!**

Have one!

It is <u>imperative</u> that you have some sort of written and signed documentation that will protect both parties in case of any differences after the deal is struck.

I can't tell you how many times I've run into vendors, even experienced ones, who have no contract or a sorely inadequate contract and apparently believe that if they ignore the need it will eventually go away. The subject of the mechanics of a contract is beyond the scope of this book. However, some trade organizations that support wedding vendors have sample form contracts with which you can start. It should specify what you are providing, where and when you are providing it, how you are providing it and how much it will cost, along with any special requirements of either party. It must be signed by both parties. A contract for goods will be different from a contract for services so be sure you use the correct format.

You must get some professional help here if you have no other means of obtaining a contract in even rudimentary form. Legal fees should be budgeted as part of your start-up costs. You might take a stab at writing a contract for your business starting with the above mentioned elements then have an attorney review it.

Once you get a contract it's important to know the meaning of each paragraph and the reason for its inclusion. From time to time you'll encounter a client who will ask you to make changes to your contract as part of the negotiations toward hiring you. There are times when you might agree to some changes, other when you won't. You must know the implications of what they are asking you to change or you might agree to something that overrides the protection your contract gives you and end up "giving away the store". There's nothing wrong with declining such a request or asking for time to consider it if you're not sure what result is being sought. Don't let a prospective client make you nervous or, worse yet, bully you into making changes you are not comfortable with or don't understand. Keep in mind that the reason for the contract is to memorialize in writing the deal you are making and it should be fair to both sides. Experienced negotiators know to ask for more than they expect and be happy with about half of what they've asked for. It works the same in contract negotiations. If you can give them some but not all of their requests they'll probably be happy. Make sure you are happy with the result as well. After all, contract negotiation is only the first part of your relationship. If you start off well, it will set the pace. A poor start can cloud the relationship for its entirety. You may even decide that you have no interest in working with the client and walk away at this stage after realizing they have a different manner of conducting business than you wish to participate in.

In my business, I have a basic form contract in my word processor, which I personalize for each client, then formally mail out. Therefore, I never have a contract with me when I interview a client. Besides thinking it looks "high pressure" to whip out a contract and a pen the moment they indicate their interest, I want the client to be sure to take the time to think about and review the agreement they are entering into. My business goal is not to book and take their money but to have a great relationship, and if they ultimately decide I'm not the best one for them I surely don't want to have the hassle of a quickly signed contract in the way of that.

OK, so you have a good contract, you have a customer who wants to hire you and asks you to send them a contract. Excellent. Send it out.

Ironclad Rule #9: DON'T SIGN YOUR CONTRACT FIRST!

Don't sign it first

I can't tell you how many vendors do that and it's a very bad business practice.

First of all, it's <u>your</u> contract and you must be in control of it at all times. Sending it out signed takes away your control as the client could make all kinds of handwritten unilateral (one-sided) changes to it that you haven't even discussed, which then become part of the contract after it's signed by both parties.

Second, and worse, you never know when your obligation to the client has started if you don't know the date the contract has been fully executed. Example, suppose the contract says you will be obligated to begin performance of your duties the day after the contract is fully signed. You will be in breach of the contract if you don't begin those duties but you won't even know when you are in breach.

Even worse, suppose you send the contract you've signed and the client never returns it to you so you assume he's not interested in your services and didn't really hire you. Suppose the wedding day comes and the client calls and says you ruined his wedding because you weren't there as contracted. You say to him that he didn't follow up with you and he says "I have the contract right here that we both have signed." Yikes. What a mess. Without a deposit (which is called consideration in the legal community) you probably would win the case, but who wants to have to defend a law suit, even a frivolous one, when you have much better things to do with your money and time than hiring an attorney and going to court.

It's just better not to leave yourself open to any thing like that if you can head it off by a simple thing like not signing your contract first.

Deposits

It's important to always get some kind of down payment when a contract is struck. In the jargon of contracts you need an offer, an acceptance and consideration before you have a contract. The consideration is usually money. How much money is left up to the contracting parties. In the wedding business it varies from minimal (maybe $100) to as much as 50% of the total fee.

Most wedding vendors have this money non-refundable per the terms of their contract.

The word "deposit" has some controversy surrounding it and vendors might variously call it "retainer fee" or "down payment" or some such term of art. Some opinions state that if it's called a "deposit" you must perform work against it and merely holding a date with it does not give you the right to keep it in case the client cancels the contract. This is a question for you to ask your attorney then choose what is right for your type of business.

Collecting

Keep in mind part of the reason you are collecting a deposit is to get a promise from the client that he or she is "investing" in your contract and thus your services. If you have held the date for them and turned away other business, they have essentially bought your time for that date. If the client cancels and you give the money back, where are you? You are out both the money and the potential for having made money from another client on that day. Not good!

Most vendors take at least 25% or better 50%. It all depends on the type of service they provide. You should always take enough to cover any outlay of time or materials that you will have made prior to the wedding day. Example by comparison: if you are a florist and have designed and produced props for the centerpieces and the client cancels the wedding, for which you have collected only $100 up front, you have just lost both the time and material for producing those props and might have turned away other business for the day, too. If you are a DJ you might not have invested anything more than some time up front since the bulk of your service is the wedding day and a few weeks prior, but you have still might have turned away other business.

Returning in case of cancellation

Any wedding cancellation is an unfortunate occurrence. There are usually high emotions involved from the client's side when their life has been turned upside down and as a vendor you, too, most probably will feel a sense of disappointment that you won't get to complete the job. The question of whether to return the down payment, or whatever you are calling it, then becomes an issue. Some vendors take a very hard line approach and follow the clause in their contract that makes the down payment non-refundable believing that, once they have taken money from a client, it's unequivocally theirs- end of story. That's not my position. I think it must be determined on a case by case basis. Certainly having the words "non-refundable" in the contract is vital and makes clear to the client from the outset that this is your position. However, if they have to cancel the contract based upon circumstances beyond their control within the first week or so after signing for a wedding that's many months away, and you have expended no time or materials and, most importantly, have not turned away other business, you might feel better about returning most if not all of what you have collected. In a case where you have put in some time and/or have begun preparations you might charge the client only for time you have put in to this point and return the remainder. It's better to take the high road in all your business dealings. You will find that your good reputation grows and you'll probably be able to sleep better at night, too.

Ironclad Rule #10: **Don't leave home without insurance!**

Insurance

This is another area of such great importance that it could be covered in the first page of this book right beside "professionalism". All businesses must have liability insurance. It matters not whether you work from your home, have a small business with a small income or work by yourself. You need it. Period.

One of the first questions I ask of a vendor who approaches me wanting referrals to my clients is whether they carry liability insurance. I am always surprised by the number of vendors who carry none. I will go no further in the conversation with them if they answer negatively. My belief is that by carrying insurance they are proving their seriousness about their business and their interest in being a professional wedding vendor. They show that they have done their homework and realize the importance of protecting both themselves and the client – and their fellow vendors - from risk.

I always shake my head in disbelief when I hear a vendor say "nothing has ever happened so I don't need insurance". I even had one say "I used to have it and nothing happened so I cancelled it because it was expensive". This is very naïve, not to mention plain stupid. First let's agree that something could happen at any time, especially on the wedding day when everything is going at a fast pace, from someone injuring himself tripping over an extension cord you have placed to your dropping and breaking an antique picture frame holding the groom's grandparents wedding photo that's being displayed. It's hard to even begin to imagine all the other unfortunate possibilities here. Why would you leave yourself open to having to make those wrongs right out of your own pocket? With liability insurance coverage your insurance carrier will go to bat for you and will go to court in your defense if something should go that far. It's like having pre-paid legal defense.

If you are sued by a client or wedding guest for an injury to person or property, your insurance company sends its lawyers in for you. Wouldn't it be awful to have to go to the trouble and expense of hiring your own legal team for that? Even without a law suit, you won't have to dig into your own pocket to pay for damages that are covered by your insurance policy once your deductible is satisfied.

Do not confuse liability insurance with errors and omissions (E&O) insurance which is more expensive coverage. That is something that few wedding vendors need as it covers you for wrong advice given. Accountants, attorneys and physicians carry such insurance for example. However, it would be a good thing to discuss it with your legal advisor or insurance agent to make sure it is not needed in your case.

Business License and Other Required Certificates

Obtain a business license if required by the local rules where you operate your business. You can usually easily get information on such requirements from your city hall or county seat.

For disciplines that require other licensing or certification, be sure to obtain them prior to opening your doors. For example a baker or candy maker must have health department clearance to sell food products to the general public, a hairdresser or manicurist must be licensed by some kind of state board and a provider of transportation must have the approval of some kind of public agency or board not to mention properly licensed drivers. Any such certification should be prominently displayed in your place of business, both to show to any inspectors that might drop by and to show to your clients who might inquire as to your credentials.

It is risky at best to conduct business without the required papers. At the minimum you could be subject to a fine. At the maximum you could have your business shut down or, I suppose, in the worst case even serve jail time.

A top wedding vendor simply does not operate without the required credentials and flying below the radar is unprofessional and places you and your client and any fellow vendors who refer you at risk. That's hardly being a team player.

Your fees and prices

What to charge when first starting out in business is always a huge question and one that should be given careful thought. You most certainly don't want to overprice your services at any stage in your career but, at the same time, you don't want to be so inexpensive that you don't make enough profit. When starting out in business you should have researched competitors in your field to get an idea of the range of prices for various services offered in your geographical area.

Many wedding vendors start at the lower end of the scale just to get jobs and get their business out in front of brides and grooms and other wedding vendors. However, pricing yourself too cheaply makes you look low end and either says you aren't very good or you are desperate for business. A slight danger in pricing your services too low is that you will begin to do weddings at that rate then you'll be referred by those brides and you'll be passed around in that level and you won't easily be able to get out of that niche.

You might consider setting the prices at the lower end of the range in which you'd like to be then offering an "introductory rate" that will put you in an even more competitive range for the time being though I am not an advocate of discounting prices (see below).

I go to a lot of networking meetings and see many new vendors. If they are dressed inappropriately I won't even consider them. (Remember you have only one chance to make a first impression). One young florist who seemed to do lovely work was dressed as if she was going to a night club with a spaghetti strap top and low jeans with her midriff bare. I tossed her card as soon as I got home as I certainly don't want a vendor who might be attired like that at a wedding.

If starting too high you may not have enough experience to compete with your higher priced counterparts and, if you do a sub-standard job because of this lack of experience, your reputation might be damaged and you'll get the "who does he think he is" feedback or worse yet, no referrals. There are some wedding vendors who want to be in the high end of the market and seem to think that charging a high price puts them on that level even though they do not conduct themselves or their business professionally and do not have the experience to warrant the prices.

Remember that at any price range or whatever niche market you are going for, professionalism is the most important component of your service. When new vendors introduce themselves to me in hopes of starting a relationship I look at their appearance, how they present themselves, their follow up and the manner in which they conduct their business. Established vendors with whom I work on a continuing basis are also evaluated, and if they don't continue to do the job as professionally as I expect I don't continue to refer them. You can see that this means you not only start out professionally but you must continue professionally.

The adage from Tom Peters, "under promise and over deliver" is one to remember.

Discounts

Once your fees are set what if someone asks you for a discount? Generally I'd say not to do it. I don't feel that wedding couples should think of vendors as bargainers that they can haggle with as I think it cheapens the vendor and the whole profession. Some communities expect it, however, and if you are in or want to work in that community, by all means do what they expect of you, but be sure to start high enough that you get what you really want and treat all your clients the same.

Discounting your prices is generally not consistent with the image of a high end wedding vendor. If a client wants you to reduce your price and you don't feel comfortable with that, you might consider offering "value added". This means holding your fee as you named it but adding some kind of service or product such as an extra solo, an extra floral arrangement, extra photos or an engagement sitting or an extra service at no charge. Just be sure you aren't giving away something that will cost you more than the requested discount.

Suppose another vendor wants you to discount your price so they can sell your services to their client then bill that client at your regular rate making the difference their profit (markup). This is not an uncommon practice in the wedding industry, but it depends on which role you want to play. If you wish to be a wholesale service and you get the bulk of your business in this way, it can work out fine. If you are primarily a direct-to-the-client (retail) business you may not want to work through someone else. However, keep in mind that anytime you get a job that you don't have to advertise for you are saving marketing dollars and effort. If you get so much work this way it might behoove you to consider it. If not, it may not be the optimal way for you to conduct your business. One thing I would avoid in any case is a dual invoice. This is where you make up an invoice to the client with one price and another invoice to a referring vendor with a different lower price in order to allow the vendor to get a kickback unbeknownst to the client. I find this deceitful and unethical.

You might have to decide on a case by case basis so stay open to what develops or make a policy that you stick with so if the question arises you know what you will do.

Changing your fees

As you become more experienced and known (and it is hoped, respected) in the wedding industry, you will most likely want to raise your prices. You should get paid more when you have more experience as you bring all prior knowledge to each job.

Periodic increases

Some wedding vendors nudge their prices up at the beginning of each year which is a natural time to do so as the start of wedding season coincides with the new calendar year in many areas. Since many vendors book as much as a year in advance it's wise to evaluate your price based on that. In mid-summer, I ask myself if I want to be working this time next year for my current fee and I tend to raise my prices then rather than at the beginning of the year. It's important to evaluate where you've obtained your business for the prior year and what kind of reactions you've gotten to your fees and the goods or services you provided. Getting feedback from former clients is the best way to know this and I have a questionnaire I send to every client after their wedding to request this feedback (see the appendix for a copy). It covers all phases of my services including fees.

You must also keep your antennae up at all times – during the job, during the planning phase and during your networking - to get a read on what's going on in your area. Trust your instinct on this, too. You'll know when it's time to change your fees. You may feel you're working too hard for the great results you provide and deserve more compensation or that you've got such a vast amount of knowledge built up that you can accomplish the job more efficiently than before or simply that it's just time to give yourself a raise.

Case by case

Changing your basic fee structure on a case by case basis is not a very good business practice and this goes along with the discussion of discounts. There is certainly nothing wrong with having a minimum charge then adding on for additional items or services as required for a particular job. This way you'll get your basic fee plus be paid fairly for additional time you spend.

Collusion

While it's important to be aware of what other like vendors in your industry are charging in your geographical area, it's also important that you not get together with those other vendors and fix prices. This is an illegal practice. However, knowing you are in the range with vendors in your same level is helpful and there is nothing wrong with discussing your fees with "competitors" or researching the market by other means. Many large corporations keep their salary levels on par with those in their industry by following surveys so it's certainly alright for small businesses to do so as well.

Overtime charges

It's important to establish a policy for overtime charges so that if the question arises you'll be prepared for it. If the nature of your work is based on hours, (such as a musician, disk jockey or limousine company, photographer or videographer) rather than being based upon a flat fee for a job (such as a florist or makeup artist) you will find that the question will arise sooner than later, especially if there is not a good wedding coordinator directing the wedding day timeline.

Each wedding has its own set of circumstances and in many cases the reception cannot be extended without advance arrangements with the venue. However, for the times it can be, know how you will handle it. If you are a venue, tell the bridal couple what the overtime charge would be per hour including the price of the room and the staff. Also tell them if it would even be possible for their event. For example, it would not be if they were the earlier wedding in a ballroom that had a later wedding for which the room must be quickly turned. If you are a music provider, tell the client the price per hour of each musician and give them a total.

> I once had a 21 piece orchestra at a wedding whose overtime rate was $8000 per hour and had the client not known in advance and been willing to pay that, it probably would have given them quite a jolt to have been charged that amount.

If you are a photographer or videographer you can collect the overtime charges upon delivery of your product, but it is important that the client is aware that overtime charges are to be incurred and you must get their authorization (written is preferable to verbal) in advance to incur them.

Several ways you can handle an anticipated overtime charge are to have a pre-authorized credit card slip signed by the client that can be relied upon in the event of extended time; collecting cash from the client on the spot; or accepting a personal check from the client. The latter can be risky as you have no recourse should the check bounce or have payment stopped which could easily happen with an unscrupulous client.

For an unanticipated overtime charge there is more uncertainty. Many wedding couples don't have large amounts of cash on them or even a blank check (should you decide to accept a check). You could ask them to sign an addendum to their contract which will make them responsible for the charge then bill then after the wedding. It is up to you and your instincts to determine the amount of trust you have with them.

There is something distasteful and mercenary about having a bride or groom have to stop as their party is in full swing to pull out a pen or wallet and do business, so I suggest having any arrangements for overtime made in advance of the wedding day.

Taxes

No one likes to pay taxes, but they are a necessity, and if you plan for them on a monthly basis the bite won't seem so large when they are due quarterly or at the end of the year. Your accountant will be able to assist you in determining how much to set aside for your income taxes and you should stay in touch with him or her during the entire year and not just at tax time.

If your business charges sales tax it's a good idea to establish a savings account into which you deposit the weekly sales tax collected. When it's time to pay the tax bill you can just withdraw what is due and send it off with your reports. You might as well be earning a little interest on that money which isn't yours anyway.

The best wedding vendors always show the amount of sales tax to be charged beginning with the first proposal. This way the client and planner know the real amount that will be out of pocket. For example, when a bride has $5000 to spend on flowers she doesn't want to have to add seven or eight percent (or whatever the local tax percentage is) to that amount because the sales tax wasn't included up front.

Be sure you know exactly how to charge sales tax, especially if you offer both a service and a product. In some states services are taxed along with products and more than one wedding vendor has had a huge and costly surprise when they discovered they should have been charging tax and hadn't been for a number of years. Besides having to come up with a large amount of money you could be accused of tax evasion. It is your responsibility as the business owner to know and obey the law.

Business systems and procedures for your office

Just as having a well written contract is a "must have" so are good business systems and office procedures. Even if you are the sole person in your business you should treat it as a large enterprise. Not only is this a good mindset toward growing the business but it will be far easier to conduct your small business while working toward attaining that growth. When you do expand it will be much easier without having to reorganize your systems.

Organization

Have you ever seen a person whose desk and office are piled high with stack after stack of papers or who has to rummage around to find something amid a sea of clutter? Remember how unprofessional it looked? That's just what you want to avoid. By having a separate, well marked (and filed!) file for every client or job, you cut out that clutter and make your business life far easier even if you have an office that no clients ever visit.

Consistency

Be consistent in the way you work with every client and every file. Have an inquiry form by your telephone (have them by all telephones if you have several) and fill it out when you get the first call asking about your services. Keep all the completed forms in another file so you can follow up if you haven't heard back from the inquiry within a reasonable length of time. It's a good idea to keep the inquiry forms even from jobs you don't get. More than once I've had a bride call after she's hired someone else with whom she became dissatisfied. After firing that planner she hired me and I was glad I had a jump on the information.

Once you have the job, immediately set up a file which is probably best kept filed by the wedding date (with a cross reference by the bride's last name if you have so many clients that you'll have difficulty finding it easily without that). Set up every file the same way so that you know right away where to find certain information when you get a phone call requesting that information. This is especially important if you have assistants or others working with you. Use divider tabs or whatever system works for you, but do it. By having the files within arms reach of your desk telephone you can have the file open in front of you (on your clean desk!) before a question is even asked and you look like a wizard to the caller because you can give them an immediate answer. It assures them that their wedding is important to you and it can even appear that you have remembered all those details. It's little things like that which subtly reinforce your professionalism. You can be in your home office in your slippers and robe and the caller imagines you in a business suit because you have come across so professionally.

Forms

Because every file will begin the same it's easier for you to have a set of forms in your computer (please get one and learn to use it if you don't have one already - your productivity and professionalism both increase with computer use) that you've created, then customize, as you begin each file. You can revise the forms and add others as often as you need to as your business evolves.

Telephones

It seems that most of us have a love/hate relationship with our telephones. They are certainly our life blood in the wedding industry but they can also be a huge annoyance.

Try to keep in mind that your telephone is for your convenience, not the caller's, and treat it as such. For example when I call someone who says "it's not a good time to talk, I'm just running out the door" I wonder why they bothered to answer. One phone rule I have is not to pick it up if I do not have at least seven minutes to talk. I would hate to have it be a prospective client that felt blown off. That's no way to make a professional first impression! A good answering machine or voice mail system with a professional message is an absolute must.

Office phones

The telephone is very often the first impression a caller gets of you or your business. Use it wisely. Have all who answer your business phone do so the same way. State the name of your business or your own name in a clear, professional manner. Always have a pad of paper and writing implement to take messages without having to ask the caller to hold on while you find that material. For calls that don't require an inquiry form I use inexpensive 3x5 scratch pads and have several by every telephone along with several pens and pencils. An office with more than one person might be equipped with spiral bound message books that provide two copies of each message. That can be helpful when having to go back to check a number for example, even months later.

The message you have on your answering machine should be treated as a marketing tool. Put as much thought into it as you do your business cards. For example, if you hear "You have reached John Doe's DJ Service. Leave your number and we'll call you back" that's a waste of time. It's obvious that you will call them back or you wouldn't have an answering machine. (One message statement I always chuckle at is "your call is very important to us". If the call was that important they'd be there to answer it!)

Instead, make a little commercial telling your callers a little about your services and how to reach you by alternate means if you have them. Example: "Thank you for calling John Doe's DJ Service, a professional DJ service offering mobile music for all ages and all occasions. We can assist you with all your DJ needs. To learn more about us before we get back to you, please visit our website at www.johndoesdjservice.com." Don't waste words on phrases like "please leave your number" – they already know to do that – when you can spend those precious seconds on promoting your business.

Some new vendors use their home phone for their business when they are first starting out. That can be fine in certain cases but never when you have other family members, especially children, answering it. Imagine if you called General Motors and a child answered. Or the receptionist asked you to wait and you heard kids crying or fighting or dogs barking in the background. Not very professional, is it? Remember, you're treating your small business as a big business and it starts right here. Do everything possible to get a phone that only you use, in a place where you can use it out of the way of everyday family life. Here again, it's better to have a machine with a good message answer your business calls than risk losing messages that a family member forgot to pass on to you or to have the caller think of you as unprofessional. The old adage "You only have one time to make a first impression" is definitely true here.

If you are on the telephone many hours of the day a headset can be a great convenience and can prevent shoulder and neck aches that come from trying to use the phone hands free. Speaker phones are generally not a good idea unless you need to make a group call and then always ask prior permission of the speaker being amplified.

As with other office equipment discussed below, be sure to get the proper telephone for your needs, whether it be a multi-line instrument, a cordless phone or a standard one-line, plug in model. There are so many telephone options available that you should easily be able to customize your telephone needs for a reasonable price.

When making or returning phone calls ALWAYS leave your number when you leave a message even if you know the recipient has your number. They might be checking their calls from a remote location and not have your number committed to memory, or may not have it close at hand. This might facilitate your getting a call back more quickly, especially if it's urgent.

Mobile phones

Mobile phones can be a boon or a bane and that varies with the circumstances – almost hour by hour sometimes! I know some vendors who have no other telephone but their mobile number and thus take all calls on it. I know others who use it intermittently with their land line.

My personal use of a mobile phone is limited to the wedding day or to times I am meeting clients who might need to get in touch with me if they are lost or late. I also check messages if I am out of the office for a long stretch and, if there is a message that needs immediate action, I place that call from my mobile discreetly and out of earshot of others so as not to annoy those around me. Because I like to gather

At one wedding I did, the officiant - a man from the bride's church - actually took a phone call as he was in the recessional (yes - the officiant!). He continued to talk during group photos of all the guests. That is what I call arrogance.

certain information from a prospective client and get it down on paper during the initial phone call, I don't use my mobile phone to take unexpected sales inquiries because I do not feel I can give my best presentation while I'm driving down the freeway or in line at the bank or at another public place. I find the latter practice an extremely annoying behavior in others. It seems that those people speak at an increased volume appearing to want to share their business with everyone. Make sure you have no ring tones at weddings! If your mobile phone must be on, set it to vibrate! Also remind the members of the wedding party to turn off their phones and pagers when you start the processional.

It's imperative that you have a mobile phone available on the wedding day in case of an emergency. Of course, you must have had the foresight to obtain the mobile number(s) of anyone you would need to contact in case of such emergency and to have given them yours as well. That would include all the vendors and certain key members of the brides and groom's families. Having the emergency numbers compiled onto a single sheet that is placed on the back of your event file is one efficient way to have those numbers at your fingertips if you should need them.

Computer, fax and other office equipment

To run a truly professional and efficient business you need certain office equipment both for your convenience and your client's convenience. Even a sole proprietor has the appearance of a large business if they conduct their business as a large business does. In the current business world you look like an amateur or hobbyist if you are not up to speed in this end.

To prepare professional looking contracts and correspondence a good computer and printer are one of the best investments you can make. You don't have to be a computer wizard to operate the basic programs for word processing or spreadsheets and you can self-teach or take classes for a few days to get at least rudimentary knowledge. Basic computers are reasonably priced so shop around and get the one that's right for you. Because technology changes so rapidly, be sure you pick one that will last you at least five years or you'll be forever upgrading.

A fax (facsimile) machine is another very important component of your office equipment. It can save untold time in communicating with clients as well as other vendors. A model that uses plain paper will be better in the long run as the film type machines produce a product that both fades over time and curls.

It is much more professional to have a line dedicated to your fax phone number. My least favorite way to use a fax is to have to call the recipient to have them flip some sort of switch before I can fax to them. This wastes my time as I often have to try several times to get through to them and if it's long distance, I incur the expense of several phone calls just to get a fax to them. My own fax line does not ring aloud so someone can fax me anytime they want to and with the dedicated line, they don't get a busy signal.

I always make a note next to any fax number I take whether it will require a pre-phone call or a cover sheet as people often use their shared office fax number and want to be sure they are there to receive it or that it will get routed to them.

In selecting your fax machine and printer consider the cost of the replacement ink cartridge before you buy as a very expensive or hard to find cartridge will eat into your profit.

E-mail

E-mail is an invaluable means of communicating with both clients and other vendors. If you are not using it you are missing an efficient business method. I have had clients living in such far-flung places as China, Japan, Taiwan and Europe, and without being able to communicate using e-mail, planning their wedding would have been next to impossible. Even for clients in your own town, e-mail is efficient because you can send letters, forms and other paperwork as attachments. You can send the same information to several parties with one e-mail that would take many extra minutes to print and send using regular mail. You can also e-mail photos which you take with a digital camera, or scan others that can be included as part of another document.

I always print the e-mails I send as well as the responses, and keep them all in the appropriate section of each client's wedding binder. I often highlight the cogent points to make it easier to find if I must go back to look something up.

When writing business e-mail the same formality and correctness of grammar is used as for a printed letter you'd send to that recipient. Save the casual language and funny graphics and bright colors for your personal e-mails. This is not to say that you can't let your business style or persona show thorough, but erring on the side of formality is more professional. Be sure to spell check your e-mails before hitting the "send" button.

Choose an e-mail address that reflects your professionalism rather than one that is too cute or silly. By having at least a hint of your company name in your e-mail address your e-mails will be less likely to be mistaken for spam and deleted. For example, which of the two following e-mail addresses would you most likely open? "CutieQ@isp.com" or "wedvendor @isp.com"?

Your business entity

Give some thought to the way in which you set up your business and consult your attorney and/or accountant before you make the decision. You can be a sole proprietor, a partnership or a corporation, of which there are several kinds. You might start off as one then change - such as first being a sole proprietor then incorporating as your business changes. As you look into the various kinds of business entities you will see that there are pros and cons to each, so get good professional advice (probably from your attorney and accountant both) that applies to your case and needs so you can make an informed decision. There will be tax implications in each business entity that you will want to consider.

Employees

As many wedding vendors do, you might start in business solo with occasional assistance from a family member. But you'll probably eventually need permanent help as your business grows. Permanent help can be part time or full time and at certain times you will need more. For example, as a solo floral designer you might be able to sell and design a big wedding but when it comes time to service it and set it up you'll need assistant florists and a delivery, set-up and strike crew. Or as a wedding planner you might be able to handle all of the in office work but you'll need an assistant or two on the day of the wedding.

It's important that these assistants be as professional as you are for they are an extension of your business. They must be attired and behave as described above even if they are only behind the scenes. You must also have them insured for both liability and worker's compensation for if they have an accident, harm someone, break something or injure themselves you will be responsible for the consequences.

Simply calling someone an independent contractor does not necessarily make them one in the eyes of the law so be sure you research that issue in advance of hiring someone and paying them cash or without withholding taxes. This is a hot button with the IRS so definitely do your homework here.

Once you have even a part time employee you will have all the issues of payroll and withholding taxes and the reports that go with that. It can be a time consuming project for a small business that seems to take on a life of its own. One suggestion is to pay your employees through a temporary service. The employee actually works for the temp service and is paid by them even though you have found them. You only have to sign their timecard, pay the temp service for the hours, taxes and an hourly premium and that's all. No government reports, accounts or numbers to worry about as the temp service does it all. Not all temporary employment services will do payroll for part-time or occasional help but with a little research you should be able to find one. The temp service I first used gave me a slightly reduced hourly rate because they did not have to screen the people I brought to them.

Once you have several employees you might find it a little less expensive to bring the payroll in house and use a payroll service that charges you a monthly fee for servicing your payroll. They will run the payroll through your business bank account and take care of all reports and tax deposits.

The type of business entity you have will often determine the best way for you to pay your employees, which might include yourself. For example if you incorporate, even as the owner of the corporation you will have to take a paycheck and get a W-2 at the end of the tax year as you will be an employee of your corporation. As a sole proprietor, in the beginning it is tempting to co-mingle your business and personal accounts, but I strongly suggest keeping them separate. If you use a credit card and don't pay your full balance every month, you'll have a horrible time tracing your expenses. The IRS doesn't look fondly upon the practice of co-mingling. See your tax and legal advisors for information on the best ways to fulfill your business needs.

For help with all things pertaining to conducting your business you can find books at your local library, take a night course in business start up at your local community college or find information through the federally sponsored Small Business Administration (SBA). These will get you started, but it's best to get and pay for good professional advice and get started in the right direction at the very beginning.

Referral Fees/ kickbacks

This is simply a loaded topic. It's also a topic that should be addressed honestly and openly as many won't discuss it or try to skirt this issue or just plain fib about what goes on in the industry.

Suppose you are in the camp that does not even want to consider giving or accepting any kind of fees or payment to or from another vendor. Then you can skip this section as you have already made up your mind about where you stand. That's perfectly fine as that is a personal business decision for which you already have an answer.

However, there are many people in the wedding industry, on both the giving and receiving sides, who struggle with the issue and I think it's a very important topic to examine openly. I think that saying "don't give them or don't take them" is just too cut and dried as it leaves no room for the nuances that arise if you examine the issue in detail.

Let's face it, an exchange of payment for business between vendors often does exist in the wedding industry (and other industries), so let's try to make some sense of it and make it a win-win-win. By that I mean a win for the paying vendor, a win for the receiving vendor and, most of all, a win for the client.

To begin with, I have met no one who can <u>clearly</u> explain the difference between a kickback, a commission, a referral fee, and a gift. It seems that most everyone has their own emotionally charged interpretation of each word depending on where they stand on the issue. Often all are lumped into the same definition which further confuses the issue

Definitions

Thus, a few definitions are in order first. I hear the terms kickback, commission and referral fee all used interchangeably. I believe they are different.

Kickback: The Random House Dictionary of the English Language says a kickback is "a percentage of income given to a person in a position of power or influence as payment for having made the income possible; usually considered improper or unethical" or "a rebate, usually given <u>secretively</u> (emphasis added) by a seller to a buyer or to one who influenced the buyer".

Black's Law Dictionary states that a kickback is "Payment back of a proportion of the purchase price to buyer or public official by seller to <u>induce purchase or to influence improperly</u> (emphasis added) future purchases......"

Commission: The Random House Dictionary says a commission is "a sum or percentage allowed to an agent, representatives, etc. <u>for their services</u>" (emphasis added).

Referral fee: While the term" referral fee" was not in the dictionary, the word "referral" is and it is defined as "a person recommended to someone or for something".

Gift: The dictionary says a gift is "something given <u>voluntarily without charge</u> (emphasis added); present".

I see nuances among the definitions particularly where I have added the emphasis.

Payment or acceptance of

As a wedding vendor should you pay money to another that sends business to you? On the reverse of that, should you as the one who sends business to another accept money from that vendor? My answer to both questions is "maybe". As mentioned above, there are those who give a flat out "no" saying the money should be returned or the savings passed on to your client but I think that's too simplistic and thus wish to examine the topic further.

Using the example of a planner and another vendor, if a payment is <u>demanded or required</u> by the planner <u>and</u> the supplier raises his/her price to accommodate that requirement <u>and</u> does not give the client a product or service worth the full value of what they have paid <u>and</u> the planner is herself charging the client a fee then the client is paying twice and that is clearly unethical. I believe this falls under the definition of a kickback. However, if the supplier is giving the client <u>full value</u> for what they are paying then it is a non-issue and could fall into the definition of a commission or a gift, or the undefined "referral fee". Example: a florist builds a ten percent referral fee into the client's $100 centerpiece and charges $110 for it. If the client is receiving a centerpiece worth $110 there is no issue. If the client receives a centerpiece worth only $100 or less this becomes an ethical question and should be avoided.

Suppose no payment is asked for by the planner but tendered freely by the supplier as a thank you. Should it be accepted or returned? When the payment of a fee for the referral is given freely by the vendor who shares his own profit with the planner I do not believe it is an issue as it is up to the vendor what he does with his profits. He may wish to give his profits to charity, buy ads in magazines or give it to those who refer him or keep it for himself for a trip to Tahiti. It's his business decision. However, if the planner feels that she wants to pass it on to her clients, that's her business decision and should be of no outsider's concern. One issue that might arise between the planner and the vendor is whether the vendor wants to give a ten percent discount to all clients brought to him by that planner, as some planners actually advertise as a means of getting business, but that is for them to resolve between themselves. The vendor may be so happy to be getting business without advertising that he will agree to such an arrangement on a regular basis.

Suppose a referral fee payment becomes merchandise or non-cash? Or is "payment" only money in the form of a check or cash? What is the difference if something has a bow around it and it's termed "a gift" versus cash in an envelope? What is the difference between a gift certificate, a bottle of champagne or cash or check given to say thank you for the business? Should all those be returned? Should any of those be returned? Does one have to disclose to their client that they got a gift other than money? What about if they get them repeatedly?

The above questions illustrate just how complex this whole concept of referral fees and gifts is and how it can even go to the ridiculous. Imagine having to tell a client that you were given a bottle of Veuve Cliquot by another vendor after you referred her wedding business to that vendor.

Commissions are very common in some wedding vendor disciplines. For example, a rental company will usually give a ten percent discount to a bona fide caterer or wedding planner to allow them to mark up the rentals while a client coming in off the street would be charged the full price. This is basically a wholesale versus retail price. Sometimes the rental company will bill the client for the rentals at full price then send the caterer the ten percent price difference in the form of a commission check after the event. There is virtually no difference in this and a florist having a wholesale and retail price of which the difference is sent to the planner as a referral fee. Again, if a planner is acting as the agent for a rental company or other vendor and bringing them business they would not have otherwise had a commission is quite in order.

Many vendors who most often deal with other vendors find it far easier to let a middle person, such as a caterer or planner, work directly with clients and feel it is worth the ten percent they pay to avoid that direct contact with clients who are often inexperienced and in need of much more direction than another wedding vendor is.

Marketing for others

Referrals from other vendors save you marketing revenue. As a vendor who gets referral business from a fellow vendor you are getting a lead that you otherwise may not have gotten. In many cases, such as from a wedding planner, this client is pre-qualified and possibly even pre-sold before being presented to you. I know of many instances where the client trusted the wedding planner so much they didn't even visit the vendor and hired that vendor sight unseen based on the planner's recommendation. Other times they have just visited the vendor to be sure they have good chemistry then hired that vendor on the spot.

Now, what in the world is wrong with the vendor giving a gift (either money or another item) to thank the planner for that business? They've been handed a good client on a silver platter for virtually no sales work on their part. As long as the contract price is not marked up from the price that anyone coming in off the street would get, I see no reason why the planner should not accept a fee from the vendor and, here's the crux of the matter, as long as the payment of the fee is not the deciding factor in the planner having sent to client there in the first place.

Now supposing, a vendor approaches a fellow vendor, in this example a wedding planner, and says, "I'll give you 10 percent of the total contract price whenever you send business to me" is this still a gift? Again, maybe. My contention is that, if, and this is the key here, IF they do not mark up their fee to give that gift to the planner, it is acceptable as it is coming from their profit and, I reiterate, it's their business what they do with their profit. However, and this is the key to the other side of the argument as stated above, IF they raise their price to give that payment it is no longer a gift, but an extra fee charged to the client. The client is then actually paying twice for the planner's service - once in the form of the fee the planner is charging them and once for the marked up fee from the vendor.

The key to all this discussion of referral fees and commissions is that the client gets the <u>full value</u> of what she is paying for no matter what else is happening in the background.

Disclosing

If you do decide to accept some form of payment from a vendor, some say it should be disclosed to your clients so they know this is being done and to prevent any suggestion of impropriety. Disclosure would take the practice out of the realm of a "kickback" as you have now removed the element of secrecy from the definition. A paragraph in your contract stating that you occasionally accept some kind of remuneration from a vendor to whom you refer your client should be adequate. If it is true, you could also add that such payment will in no way influence such referrals. Because I do not let the payment or non-payment of referral fees influence my decision to whom I refer my clients, I have included that phrase in my contract. And it is absolutely true. As an example, the music provider whom I refer first virtually all of the time does not and has never paid a percentage and never will but they are so fabulous and I love to have them on my team so much that it is a non-issue. See your legal advisor regarding any wording you wish to include in your contract.

Another school of thought is that there is no need to disclose it at all as it's strictly a business transaction between the payer and receiver and thus not of concern to a third party-client. You will have to ascertain your own position on that question and, again, seek the advice of your legal counsel.

Ethics

Conducting your business with the highest ethics will get you a long way. Your reputation is your most valuable business asset. Much of that reputation rests on your ethics and how you are perceived among your peers and clients as it defines who you are to those around you.

"There is no such thing as a minor lapse of integrity."

Tom Peters

So what exactly are ethics?

Definition

The dictionary definition states that *ethics* are 1. a system of moral principles 2. the rules of conduct recognized in respect to a particular class of human actions or a particular group, culture, etc. 3. moral principles, as of an individual.

The definition of *ethical* states 1. pertaining to or dealing with morals or the principles of morality; pertaining to right and wrong conduct. 2. in accordance with the rules or standards for right conduct or practice, esp. the standards of a profession.

To state "be ethical in all your business dealings" is a good beginning but doesn't say enough. People's interpretation of "ethical" can differ based upon their background, their experience or their culture. Or they can think "I'm within my rights" or "it's legal" to do a certain act while they are actually violating the spirit of the law if not the letter of the law.

A blatant example is the guy who establishes his own church (he's the only member) and uses it to raise money (lots of it) for some appealing cause, then spends it all on luxury items for himself. Clearly he's within the law to establish a church. However, the spirit of the law does not contemplate him establishing a church for such a purpose. Ethical people would agree that this guy isn't among them.

Each of us has to decide where we wish to be on the ethical scale and there is sometimes a fine line between ethical behavior and sullied behavior.

Sometimes we make the wrong decision in the process of learning or finding the place where we feel most comfortable. It's always best to take the high road. And certainly if we do make a mistake we can always go back and try to rectify it with at least an apology (even if it is years later). In deciding on a certain issue that might have a difficult answer maybe a good yardstick to measure your options would be "could I look my grandmother in the eye and tell her I did this?"

An early example of taking credit for work not your own was a Christmas home wedding I coordinated in the groom's mom's home. Realizing she was becoming overwhelmed she hired me to come on board after some of the plans had already gotten underway. This included draining and scaffolding the swimming pool and arranging for a tent in back yard. I referred a caterer and a décor designer among other things and was very much involved in the design of both the menu and the decor. In a newsletter sent out by the caterer a few months later there was a story in a section they called "Parties of Note" in which they described the entire event as if they had done it all from the start. There was no mention whatsoever of the décor designer or me as they took credit for the whole event! Guess who I have never referred since. (What further amazes me is that this caterer never called me to inquire why I stopped referring them. I guess they didn't need or want any more business.)

Lena Malouf, one of the most talented and well-known international event designers and former International President of ISES, said during a recent lecture, "If you're going to survive in business you have to do the right thing twenty-four hours per day." It is up to you to determine for yourself just what that means for you and then practice it religiously.

Specify what is and isn't ethical

While the study of ethics is an entire course at the university level and is well beyond the scope of this book, we can at least look at some examples of less than ethical behavior in the wedding business.

Bashing competition

When meeting a prospective client don't run down your competition, especially by name. Most clients are very uncomfortable with this and it does nothing positive for your sales pitch or your image. Work on your sales pitch to show them how you will give them better value without having to resort to such negative marketing tactics.

Taking credit for work that isn't yours

Never try to pass off someone else's work as yours or take credit for something you did not do.

Pricing from another vendor's proposal

Sometimes a bride will bring a proposal from a competing vendor and ask you to beat the price. Refuse to do that. In fact don't even look at that other proposal. Return it to the bride as you politely explain that such behavior is not in keeping with your business standards and that it is unethical for you to take someone else's ideas and copy them for a cheaper price. As tempting as it might be, a top wedding vendor will <u>never</u> do it. Offering to do your own design and proposal is a way for you to present your work for the client's consideration and she may find your creativity and talent outshine the prior proposal. If not, do you want to work with a client who herself has shaky ethics? In all fairness to the imaginary client just discussed, it may not have occurred to her that this is improper behavior and once she is aware of your position she will likely understand and possibly will raise her own level of standards at least a small degree.

Exaggerating your qualifications

There is not a thing wrong with bragging about yourself and your qualifications a little bit (as long as you don't become obnoxious!). After all, when you've worked hard to get where you are you should be proud of yourself. However, exaggerating or just plain lying about your qualifications is unethical. I have seen too many vendors stretch the truth about their experience, training or qualifications. While your clients may never know, your peers might. Any tarnish on your reputation is to be avoided.

There are endless other examples of unethical behavior but in the end it is up to you to decide your position which, it is hoped, will be the highest level of ethics. As more and more wedding professionals are aware of, and practice, the highest ethics they soon become the norm and less ethical vendors will be drummed out of the industry. It's up to us collectively to do this.

Complaints and Unhappy Clients

The more weddings you are involved in the greater the chance you will eventually have a complaint or an unhappy customer. As much as you try to make every wedding you are involved in the best one yet, the law of averages says something, either minor or major will eventually go wrong and often it will be beyond your control. So it's best to determine in advance what your policy will be in when that happens. Some vendors have so firmly determined their policy in advance that they advertise it such as saying something like "One hundred percent satisfaction or your money back".

Will you refund the entire fee paid by the unhappy client? Will you refund a part of the client's fee? Will you do the finished product over again (for a wedding this is often an impossibility as the wedding obviously cannot be restaged).The degree of severity of the wedding element that went awry will determine just what you will do to make it right for both the client and yourself and will have to be considered on a case by case basis even with a pre-determined policy.

One photographer with whom I work had an extremely particular bride who ordered two large, identical albums. When the second one came, the bride said it was different. Only when they were side by side could one discern a slight color variation. The photographer went into problem solving mode and worked tirelessly with the bride to remake the album to her satisfaction and though he probably lost money on it, her satisfaction was his prime concern. In the end she was delighted and he was as well. His esteem in my eyes also went sky high and I have shared that information about him with many others.

Your image and your reputation rest on your policy. An old adage goes something like "a happy customer will tell another, an unhappy customer will tell everyone". It's always best to head off the unhappy customer in hopes that they will download to you first so you can correct the error- whether it's real or perceived - and make it right by or at least formally apologize to the client if nothing else can be done.

Unfortunately there are a few clients that will find fault where there is none, or where they played a part in what they see as the negative outcome, but they will have to be treated as legitimate and their complaints handled as graciously and quickly as all others.

Once you are sure that you have done all you can do to rectify the issue, whether it's by a full or partial refund, a replacement of an item or a formal apology, it's important that you learn from the mistake or incident. Change anything about the way you are currently doing business to avoid such an occurrence in the future then let it go and continue to move forward. It's not just the incident and its occurrence but the speed and manner in which you handle it that will determine your reputation and whether fellow vendors will refer you again.

If the occurrence is of such severity that your insurance company or attorney needs to be involved, contact them immediately and let them handle the negotiations then follow their direction as to your involvement. They may require that you have no further communications with the client until the case is settled. See the section on Insurance for a discussion of the importance of carrying liability insurance.

> One bride's family hired a fun trolley type vehicle to move their large wedding party from the church to the reception. The father of the bride had inspected the trolley in advance and was very excited about it. The day of the wedding the passengers claimed the driver was using the automatic shift as if it was a stick shift causing the passengers to fall out of their seats and gifts to fly around. Dad also stated that it was a different vehicle than he had inspected. Strong letters of complaint were sent the following Monday. After much discussion with the trolley owner and operator which included a test ride in which nothing was determined to be faulty with the equipment or the driver's ability, the company's decision was to refund the entire fee for the trolley rental. Without admitting any wrongdoing and truly believing there was none, they simply felt that it was not worth tarnishing their reputation by arguing over a subjective matter. They felt that, if the client's perception was that is was a bumpy ride that was unpleasant for them and their guests, then it was and they made it good.

Marketing, Sales, Advertising and Publicity

Without people knowing about you and your business it is difficult to stay in business. It's as simple as that. That doesn't necessarily mean you have to take out full page ads in all the wedding magazines or try to outspend your perceived competition to get better known than they. What it means is making people, both prospective clients and other wedding vendors, aware of you and your product or service.

Marketing

Everything you do related to your business should be considered a marketing opportunity, from how your telephone is answered to the way you conduct yourself while working at a wedding. It is your business persona. It's the picture of yourself or your business that you want people to think of when your name is mentioned. It's fashionable today to call it your brand.

Some new business people think that advertising is marketing when it is actually just one component of it. Marketing is the broader picture and will encompass the entire brand or persona you are building, while advertising exemplifies your brand which becomes your image.

Your image is built slowly, but it must be consistent. There are many good books that explain in detail how to go about building your image, but on a rudimentary level the following, several of which have already been discussed in more detail in the sections above entitled "Professionalism" and "Conducting Business", should be considered:

Your appearance

Always dress as you want to be perceived by your peers and your clients. Make sure your apparel and grooming are consistent with that of a top wedding vendor and with the brand you wish to convey.

At a recent meeting of wedding consultants and various wedding vendors that numbered about 200 "professionals" I saw diverse attire from business suits to blue jeans and a too tight spaghetti strapped jumpsuit - both of the latter are inappropriate for a business meeting. The big question in my mind when I see something like that is "what are they thinking".

Your behavior

Manners and the way in which you present and conduct yourself are a big factor in building your image. If you aren't comfortable with your knowledge of etiquette you'll find plenty of books on the subject that will help you build confidence and teach you manners for both business and social occasions.

Your associates and clients

The old adage "tell me who your friends are and I'll tell you what you are" is often on the mark. Associating with the kinds of people you wish to be like can bring you to more of that kind. Just be sure you are truly qualified to be part of the league in which you wish to play or you could come off looking like a "wannabe" or get in over your head which could ultimately harm your reputation.

Your business cards and stationery and brochure or other collateral pieces

As simple a thing as your business card is advertising material and gives an immediate impression of who you are (or want to be) to the recipient. Make sure all printed pieces you use are well designed and of the quality consistent with a top wedding vendor. A carefully chosen logo that is carried on all pieces of your stationery and marketing material and included in all of your advertising is an important factor in building your brand. A gaudy or poorly designed card with too much information can be a turn off. A computer generated business card or brochure can work but they usually look home made, especially if the paper is too thin.

Your telephone message

Your telephone message is often the very first contact a prospective client will have with you so make it a nice little sales pitch and always refer the caller to your website (you do have one, don't you?) so they can visit that between the time they leave you a message and you call them back.

Your website

A website is a wonderful sales tool and should reflect your image as well or better than any other marketing tool you use. It should be current, so update it often. It is generally far quicker and much less costly to update your website than it is to reprint brochures so find a good and reasonably priced web master (unless you are capable of and have the time to do that yourself). It will be studied by prospective clients and passed to others and often printed for their reference, so be sure it conveys exactly what you want it to convey in both the image and information departments.

Always keep the information on your website current or it could work against you. Including too many graphics that will slow the opening or loading of the site that can cause viewers to get impatient and leave before they've seen as much as you'd like them to. Too many gimmicks can be a turn off to viewers so be sure you are showing them what you want them to know about your business. The web designer doesn't have to include every bell and whistle he knows to prove his ability.

Your portfolio

The minute you begin your business, or starting right now if you are already an established business, begin compiling your marketing portfolio. It will become an invaluable sales tool that is totally unique to your business.

What exactly is a marketing portfolio? It is a binder, album or case that holds a group of mounted or laminated photos and other information that is shown to a prospective client during your initial sales meeting to illustrate examples of your creativity and experience in the field.

It is not a scrapbook of ideas that you've pulled out of magazines – something like that can be used once you've begun working together to design the wedding if you like – nor is it things you wish you'd done or think you could do. Rather, it is examples of your prior work along with, perhaps, copies of publicity you have received, thank you letters from former clients and vendors you've worked with (these become testimonials to your talent, ability to be part of a team or whatever points you care to emphasize to a prospective client). It should also include a copy of your insurance certificate and business license and other credentials such as certificates from training courses you've taken relating to your field of specialization. In short, it must be dynamite!

The examples of your work can be in a good quality photograph or actual samples or both. For example a floral designer or linen rental company should have professional photos of a wedding showing their product in use. A makeup artist or hair dresser should show photos of actual brides on their wedding day for whom they've provided the makeup or hair services. A provider of favors or invitations could show actual samples of their product as well as photos of them in use.

Having your portfolio in a nice, professional looking book of some kind shows it off to the best advantage. Please do not have piles of unorganized photos for a client to look at or albums that are falling apart from overuse. This creates the impression that you are sloppy and unorganized and causes the client to wonder if you really can pull off what you say you can. Don't try to use the excuse that you are creative so therefore the left side of your brain doesn't work. Get someone with a left brain to help you if necessary. Remember you only have one time to make a first impression and this is a critical one. Sloppiness and disorganization are not consistent with being a top wedding vendor.

If you're new in business you might be asking where you are supposed to get the photos for your portfolio. At first take them with your own camera and crop them and/or enlarge them to show what you'd like your clients to see. Pick out only the best shots that illustrate your best work. Fewer really good photos are better than many mediocre ones. Contact the professional photographer of the wedding in advance and ask him or her if they could take a few shots suitable for your needs as part of their job on the wedding day. Make it clear to them that you expect to pay for those shots then be sure to follow up within a reasonable time to see the proofs and place your order. Many forward thinking photographers will give those photos to you as an advertisement for themselves, but don't expect that, especially if you have no relationship with them.

I suggest having a portfolio that is loose-leaf. That way you can constantly update it with new and better examples of your work. When I think of the first portfolio I put together compared to the one I have now it's night and day, but I had to start somewhere just as we all do, and it did the job for me.

Maybe you're thinking "My line of work doesn't lend itself to a portfolio." Nonsense. Every wedding discipline can have some kind of portfolio with all the paperwork described above and a few photos of them or their staff on the job. For example if you own a bartending service you can show photos of your workers on the job in their uniforms behind a bar as your client will see it at their wedding. If you are an officiant, photos of yourself performing an actual wedding ceremony can be included to illustrate how you dress for a wedding.

Ironclad Rule #11: NEVER take credit for work that is not your own.

NEVER place photos of another person's work in your portfolio. This is a huge breach of ethics besides being a misrepresentation.

Your "elevator speech"

Develop a pithy one -line "speech" that succinctly describes your business in such a way that you can state it during the time it takes an elevator to go a few floors. You should leave your listener wanting to know more. As an example, one special events business coach when asked what her line of work is says "I help people double their business". Whose attention wouldn't be grabbed by that statement?

Work on your "elevator speech' and let it become such a part of you that it rolls off your tongue whenever anyone at a party,

> There was a newly established caterer in a town near me who came in with a big splash sending expensive and beautiful marketing material and contacting planners and venues to introduce themselves to the wedding and event community. Upon examination of their brochure, which implied that the photos were of their work, it became clear that every photo was copied from a well known wedding book. When the company folded after about a year I wondered if their lack of ethics had anything to do with it.

at a networking function (or in an elevator) asks you what you do. You'll love the reaction and have a great opener to describe your business in more detail.

Sales

Many people shrink from the idea of selling something, saying they're not good at it or they are embarrassed to do it. However, you cannot be successful in business without selling your product, whether it's a tangible item or your time. Selling doesn't have to be cold-calling or high-pressure tactics that we see caricatured in movies. It is showing and/or telling your prospective clients how you can help them find a solution to a current "problem" they have. The "problem" could be the need for a videographer at their wedding and you, as a videographer, must show them that you are the best person to solve it.

You might be one of three or four vendors presenting your pitch to a client, as that is the usual number propounded by bridal magazines or planners. Here is your opportunity to present yourself at your best and to demonstrate to the client that you can and will do the best job for them. Some clients will hire the first person they interview and even cancel other appointments they might have if they find what they want right away. Others will want to interview everyone they can find. If you ultimately are not the one chosen you should review your presentation in your mind to see what you can improve the next time, especially if you thought you were right for the job and conducted a good interview. You can always ask the client why they didn't choose you. Most are happy to talk to you about it and you can get invaluable tips from them. If they won't talk to you, that's fine, too. Nothing is lost by inquiring and much could be gained.

Sometimes you will conclude that the client and you are not a good fit, and there's not a thing wrong with turning down a job if you see yellow flags during the interview process. Perhaps they have unrealistic expectations with the budget they have, perhaps their personality is abrasive or perhaps you don't feel qualified to handle their wedding. Being forthright at the outset is better than suffering later and risking your reputation if it doesn't work out well.

The mechanics of selling are well beyond the scope of this book, but there are dozens of books and seminars where you can learn or sharpen your skills. There are different styles of selling and you should find the method that best suits your image and personality then further refine it to a level where you are comfortable. Enlist a friend to help you practice your sales pitch and in time you'll develop a great one.

As you go through each day observe how businesses sell to you and use this as inspiration for how you will sell to your clients. What turns you off and what makes you want to buy? Adapt their methods to your business and stay open to new ideas that could work for you.

Advertising

Advertising can be a very costly proposition, especially for a small or new business, and it's very important that you spend those dollars wisely. Most small businesses don't have the luxury of hiring an ad agency so must rely on their own ingenuity. The old standby "Guerilla Marketing" by Jay Conrad Levinson is a great book with some amazing ideas that can be adapted to any type of business.

I love it when I ask a prospective client how she heard about me and she says something like, "I'm not sure, I see your name everywhere" as that means my marketing and the little advertising I do have reach.

Where to advertise

Often, the first place we think of advertising is in a magazine or the yellow pages. However, print ads in magazines are very costly and you have to wait for their appearance. Additionally, they are often not as effective as you might like them to be because of the "frequency factor" which says that a prospective client must see your ad half a dozen times before knowing you. In other words, a one time shot in a magazine probably isn't the best way to spend your advertising dollars.

The yellow pages can be good for some businesses and not for others. Some perceive the yellow pages as attracting a lower end client but I believe it depends on the ad you run. My own ad is a single line with my business name and telephone number followed by my web address. I get about one or two really good weddings each year from the yellow pages and for the small expense of the ad I think it's worth it to have my name out there.

One of the most effective ways of getting known in your business is networking, which will be covered in depth in the next section. When a new vendor, or an established one who is ramping up their advertising, asks me for advice on placing an ad here or there, I ask them, "how many strategic people can you take to lunch with that money?" By this I mean it probably would be more effective to build a one-on-one relationship with several key people who would repeatedly refer clients to you than to do a shotgun approach to advertising and hope to hit some prospective clients in the process.

After all, repeat business is about relationship building. But, you say, a bride only comes to you once, how is that going to give you repeat business? The other vendors you work with and even the bride's family and friends are potential repeat business so should be treated as such.

Certain venues have lists they call "Preferred Vendors" or something similar. In some instances they charge you to be on that list. In the area where I work there is an outside publishing company that handles this for a venue that contracts with them to put together a booklet. I am not a fan of this type of list or any concept of paying to be listed because it clouds the issue of whether a listed vendor is referred because they are outstanding in their field or merely one who is willing to pay for the listing. The listing venue loses control of the quality of their vendors as they cannot remove them, if necessary, until the ad period (usually one year) is over.

A "real" preferred vendor list can be an excellent way for you to meet pre-qualified clients and you must treat your listing as a privilege, keeping in mind that the venue can remove your name at will if the quality of your work does not continue to be up to par.

Being included in such a preferred list is not as simple as calling the catering director of the venue and asking to be on the list. Imagine how many calls they get from interested vendors who they have never heard of. Most venues, especially the highest-end ones, cannot or do not want to stick their neck out and recommend an unknown vendor or, even worse, a vendor with a poor reputation. Here's where building relationships comes in, again.

How much to spend?

While some experts advise that you should spend between five and ten percent of your gross income on overall marketing, there is no strict formula for determining how much advertising you should do or where you should do it. You'll have to try various methods and places and see which work for you. As a rule of thumb, I suggest being conservative in spending money on it when you are first starting out and lightly testing the waters before making a huge plunge. People who sell ads are first and foremost salespeople and, while it might seem that they have your interest at heart, you must remember that they are most interested in filling their ad space. So be sure what they are selling really is right for you before you commit.

It's very important to always ask a new contact where they heard about you so you can keep track of the results of your ads' effectiveness. Then not only keep track of it, but evaluate it as well. Think hard before you renew an ad if you haven't had the expected results or it doesn't prove to be as profitable as it should have been.

Getting publicity

Publicity is a wonderful thing and it's most often free! Try your hardest to get your name out there by means of free publicity. (But, please, never become a pest in the process.) Let reporters know you are available to be an expert quoted in their publication. Send press releases for awards you've won, for new services you're offering and for promotions or remarkable additions to your staff. All might not be printed, but some will, and it's just another way for your name to get out there. There are those who believe that no publicity is bad publicity as long as your name is out there. This might be true and certainly as long as you are conducting yourself and your business is a professional manner, there is little danger of bad publicity anyway.

Some people are afraid to talk to the press for fear of being misquoted. Of course, there is always a danger of that. I suggest that you choose your answers to their questions carefully and also that you make sure you aren't saying something "off the record" that will be attributed to you anyway. Remember, reporters are looking for a pithy statement. They like unusual or revealing information. That's what sells their publications.

The mechanics of "getting press" is beyond the scope of this book but there are articles and books on the subject at the library.

Making a Niche

What is a niche? It's a specialty for which you are known in your field and can often be so well defined that when someone thinks of you they immediately picture your niche. An example is a wedding planner who specializes in waterfront weddings or a DJ who specializes in short notice jobs by being packed and able to be there in less than an hour and can save the day when a scheduled DJ fails to arrive.

It is a good thing to develop a niche and you can do so in any field. It doesn't have to be the only thing you do (in fact it probably shouldn't be), but it can bring you a lot of business. You could even parlay your niche into a speaking career or one in which you teach others if you are so inclined.

"Nichecraft" by Dr. Lynda Falkenstein is a well known book that will give you guidance in finding and establishing your niche.

Giving Back

Donations

From time to time non-profit or other community groups will approach you to donate something for a raffle, a silent auction or other fund-raising event. They might offer to print your name or business card in a program or on their advertising material in exchange for your donation.

It's always nice to support your community and the good they are doing but you must think about such donations and examine how much good you are doing and what benefit you will get as a small business owner besides just being kind-hearted. The funds to support such donations should be considered part of your advertising budget and the results expected should be commensurate with your marketing plan. Too many spontaneous giveaways with no results will put a strain on your marketing dollars and could leave you with no money for your real marketing plan.

Keep in mind that many of the groups asking for donations will be small and, while your name might be printed on their marketing material, there will be a narrow distribution resulting in few people seeing it and even fewer acting upon it.

When making your marketing plan, include a reasonable portion of it for donations if that is something you'd like to participate in. Then dole it out according to the plan and, when it's gone for the year, turn down any further requests. That way you can do your civic duty and stay within the marketing parameters you have set for your business. If there is a recurring donation you like to make each year it can easily be incorporated into your marketing plan at the beginning of each year.

You don't have to give something to every group that asks. It's important to evaluate whether you really support the cause of the recipient group and might have given them a donation anyway. After all if your company name is connected with the group you will be identified with it.

Mentoring

The more successful and well known you become the more people will ask things of you. It seems that everyone wants a piece of your success. It's important to give back to your community and to the profession that gave you success but you must learn to be selective or you could find yourself being taken advantage of or stretched very thin. Time is usually a scarce commodity.

Besides giving money or product donations to a cause in which you believe, a good way to give back is to mentor someone who is interested in your line of work. Your local high school or college might have a mentoring or intern program or you might find someone through a trade organization. The intern/mentee might have no experience in your field but would like to shadow you for a day or so to see first hand what you really do. They might have taken a course of study and have a required number of hours of practical work to complete the requirements for a certificate. No matter the situation, an intern or mentee must adhere to the high standards of your company, as they are an extension of it while accompanying you at work. You have every right to expect the same from them as you would from an employee which will include your dress and conduct code among other things.

If an intern/mentee accompanies you to client and/or vendor meetings, you must request approval in advance from those with whom you are meeting. Most people will not hesitate to welcome an intern/mentee when asked but there is an occasional client or vendor who will not agree to have someone else sit in.

Networking and Public Speaking

Networking

Ah, networking. It's probably the single most important way to get known in the business community. It's not necessarily a direct means of getting clients or jobs, but meeting and getting to know other business people, especially in the wedding industry, is very much worth the time you spend doing it. However, there is definitely a right way to do it.

To begin with,

Ironclad Rule #12 - NEVER leave home without your business cards.

Have them in the jacket pocket of every single one of your business suits and have them placed inside those pockets so that when you pull one out to hand it to someone it is facing upwards and toward the recipient. That is, after all, your first line of marketing and you want it to give the best first impression it can, however subtle. Also carry a small supplemental supply of cards in your wallet, briefcase or glove compartment so you are never very far from them. On more than one occasion I've had vendors ask for a stack of my cards so they could display them in their shop and being able to pull 10 or 15 cards out on the spot gave me a little marketing edge.

If you are at a networking meeting and are invited to wear a nametag be sure to place that nametag just below your <u>right</u> shoulder so those you are meeting can look directly at your name as you offer your hand for a shake. I always find it silly when someone places their nametag at waist level or removes their jacket without repositioning their name tag. Be sure to use your full name and the name of your business on your name tag. The object of networking is to become known so give those you are meeting every opportunity to know who you are. Why spend the time going out trying to get known when no one can see your name or your company's name?

You must plan your networking attack and not just go out meeting people for the sake of doing it, though that won't hurt you in the long run. It's just more effective to plan it. When you have learned how to network you will instinctively be better at it. There's a learning curve and a comfort level with this, just as with anything else.

Attending Chamber of Commerce mixers and meetings is one way to start, especially if you have a store front. Home based business might not benefit as much since most chambers focus on the shops and front row businesses, but if you are active in the group you will become known. International groups that are especially affiliated with the wedding or special event industry such as ABC (The Association of Bridal Consultants) or ISES (International Special Events Society) are great because all participants are a potential relationship for you. You must attend regularly and if you are active in the leadership of the group you will get much more out of it, in addition to becoming better known.

> One new videographer I met at a networking meeting was lamenting the fact that he had taken 14 business cards from wedding coordinators at a prior meeting. He'd sent out 14 marketing letters and only got two phone calls back. He naively believed that one meeting would turn into business galore. I explained that he needed to build relationships and it would take time.

I always wonder why a new vendor thinks he can drop by a meeting once with a stack of business cards and believe that doing so will get him a rash of new clients. By its definition there is no way one can build a relationship based on one encounter.

A word of caution as you attend networking meetings and mixers: wine or other alcoholic beverages are often served as part of the refreshments. Be careful of the amount you consume - if any. Consider networking part of your job and remember that you are making an impression on those you meet. Waving a glass around while talking sends the wrong message and slurring your words is not the impression to give to someone with whom you hope establish a professional relationship. I have put several vendors on my personal "do not refer" list based upon their behavior at networking meetings. My own rule is not to drink alcoholic beverages at all when I am at networking meetings as I consider it the same as being at work.

When you are new to the wedding business you will likely not know many other vendors. When you hear of a vendor that you think might be a good contact for you, do a little research by looking at their web site or browsing their shop if they have one. If you like what you see, call and introduce yourself and ask about the product or service they have. Focus on learning about them. This is not a marketing call with the purpose of telling them about yourself or your business. It is an educational call for you to learn about them. If they ask you about your service or product, fine, give them the information they seek, but don't launch into a marketing speech, as that's not the purpose of the contact. They might have a brochure that you're interested in so request one for your files.

Once you have determined that this could be a good relationship to pursue it's a good idea to meet them in person. Call to ask if you can take a little of their time to learn more about their service or product. An astute vendor whom you approach in this way will know the value of establishing a relationship with another vendor and probably will consent to this - especially if you contact him at a less busy time. You must be careful not to be a pest. Make your visit a short one with the focus of learning about their service or product so you can consider utilizing their services.

Carefully consider the time you are calling. For example, I do not like being called for either networking or marketing purposes on a Monday morning when I'm trying to get my desk and thoughts in order for the week ahead and most wedding vendors are very busy at the end of the week while prepping for the weekend's weddings. Many wedding vendors take Mondays off to recover from weekend work so Tuesday might not be the best day to contact them either.

At this point, I would suggest not visiting your direct competitors. When a new kid on the block comes around it might be interpreted as spying and that's not the first impression to convey. Of course, you should know what your competitors are up to. You should have thoroughly researched them prior to establishing your business and you should stay on top of what they are doing but you must be discreet.

Public speaking

The words "public speaking" might send shudders down your spine. It has been said that speaking before a group is one of the most feared things many people can imagine. But as a business person it behooves you to tackle this fear and become at least semi-proficient. You might argue that as a florist, invitation vendor, favor supplier or (fill in the blank here) you'll be behind the scenes and don't need to speak publicly. That is simply a cop out. First, at many networking groups you will be called upon to introduce yourself and give a description of your business. If you don't speak properly you're losing a great mini-marketing opportunity and the ability to make a great first impression. Remember you're reading this book because you want to be a top wedding vendor – not a mediocre one. There are plenty of the latter already. Anyone can be mediocre, but to rise to the top you must be able to speak well before a group and the confidence you will have developed carries over to all phases of your business.

Even doing a presentation to clients is a form of public speaking. You might have the bride and groom and a parent or two along with a wedding planner grilling you with questions about the décor you are showing or what your services will consist of, so knowing how to organize your thoughts for the presentation and then thinking on your feet as questions arise is very important.

Further, as you become well known in the wedding industry you'll likely be called upon to speak before a group. This could be a group of your peers as a panelist or maybe when you accept an award. You certainly don't want to botch either of those because of fear of public speaking.

How do you become a confident speaker? The most universal method is to join a group called Toastmaster's International. It is a group of people from all walks of life who meet in an organized fashion to share the common interest of becoming better public speakers. There are groups in most cities and many communities all over the world. They meet at varied hours of the day from breakfast to evening. Many large corporations have a club on their property and many invite outsiders to participate.

As you proceed along a prescribed path through printed material provided by the organization you will be amazed at how good you'll get in a short time. For more information on Toastmaster's visit their website at www.toastmasters.org. I've been a member of several clubs over the years and have found them to be a nurturing atmosphere for an emerging orator. There are even clubs who videotape your speech so you can really see how you appear to others.

There are other ways of becoming a good speaker, such as just doing it and learning as you go or hiring a coach. If these methods are better for you then pursue them. Do whatever it takes to get over the public speaking hurdle. It will stand you in good stead in both your personal and business lives.

Competition

There are wedding vendors of all kinds who think that anyone else in their field is "competition". I don't believe that. I think that another vendor in your field is just another person or business that's doing the same thing you're doing and the one who is doing it best is the one who gets the best jobs. If you conduct your business out of fear of the competition you're wasting your energy and possibly hindering the growth of your business. Looking over your shoulder all the time forces you to focus on them and not on you and your clients.

This is not to say that you should ignore others in your field. You must always know basically what they are doing, but you must approach it from an informational angle rather than a fear angle. Personally getting acquainted with others in your field by networking at trade organizations or just contacting them to introduce yourself helps bring a healthy business climate to the wedding community. Having open communication with them provides you with yet another relationship that can contribute toward your great reputation. You'll often gain another resource. I can't tell you how many times a fellow wedding planner has called me asking for a referral for another vendor. I'm always happy to give them that information. Then when I need such help I can call upon them.

There is enough business to go around, especially for the best vendors. In fact, you'll find as you get a sterling reputation and your business grows that you'll have to turn business away. By being friendly with others in your field you'll know someone who does high quality work and can feel comfortable referring your overflow to them. They, in turn, will refer you if they are booked.

From time to time you, as an established vendor, will get calls from someone just starting in the business wanting to understudy you. Some will be so blatant as to ask that they be taught everything you know so they can become as good as you are. It always surprises me to hear that request and I wonder why they think anyone should do that for them. It probably took years of trial and error and study, not to mention financial investment, to get to your level of success and they expect you to hand it to them with the minimum of work.

While mentoring someone can be a satisfying way to share, there is no particular virtue in "giving away the store". Approaching an established vendor in this way can be a turnoff that will slam doors rather than unlock them. You must approach it as a job shadow for a day or volunteer your services to them. In other words, what will you give them in return for the information and the opportunity you'll get from them?

By the way, I don't suggest that you or a friend call a competitor and pose as a bride to ask their prices or find out how they work. While some consider it market research, I consider it deceit. I'd rather have someone call me and state they are trying to become a wedding planner and ask me how I charge than to waste my time in a non-productive game. In fact, I can often spot a shopping call.

Some wedding coordinators say they don't want to give out the names of their resources because those vendors will get too busy and won't be available when they need them. That line of reasoning is absurd. Unless you can give your favorite vendors enough exclusive business so that they don't have to work for anyone else, how do you expect them to stay in business and even be there the next time you need them? I'd rather see my best vendors working and becoming more successful, too.

You get back what you give. That's a pretty simple statement but it is true. It's amazing the great reputation you'll get when you help others by sharing with them. You'll also get willingness from them to help when you need it.

Wedding Design

The design of the wedding is the end result that the guests see. It is the beautiful part that creates the memories that linger in photographs and videos. It's also the part that is perceived as "fun" by observers who have a soft spot for weddings and who may not realize how much planning, organization and plain hard work go into making all the "fun".

Developing a sense of style and design

Whether you are part of the creative team of a wedding such as a florist or lighting vendor, or are a part in the non-creative side of a wedding such as a limousine driver, you must have a sense of style. Remember, a wedding is a form of show business and the entire event must be packaged as such. It's important for all vendor participants to catch the vision and mood of the show and operate within that vision and mood even if it's in as simple a way as how your staff is dressed.

If you are on the creative side of a wedding, your sense of style and design are ultra important and will no doubt play an important role in landing your clients. Style does not mean flamboyancy or histrionic behavior a la Franck in the now classic movie "Father of The Bride", though he definitely has a distinct style. It means having a sense of aesthetics and taste appropriate to the occasion. It means giving a new twist to an old method. If you don't have it naturally it can be developed or honed by training and observation.

Training can be classes offered in design or art at your local junior college. It can be working with an experienced designer who imparts that knowledge to you. It can be doing it and learning by trial and error what works well and what doesn't work so well.

Observation can be attending art exhibits and fashion events or visiting design houses or even model homes. It can be noting how finer establishments that are known for their service, such as Neiman-Marcus and the Ritz-Carlton, display their goods or treat guests. It can be reading magazines to watch the latest trends.

For designing weddings

There are probably dozens of books and magazines chock full of photos of beautiful weddings. These can be a great inspiration to a designer. Not to copy certainly, but to see what the fertile imaginations of others come up with. "Think outside the box" is an overused cliché by now, but there is a lot of truth in it from a design standpoint. You've got to see things in different ways that can give you solutions to challenges you may encounter. Like the wonderful buffet table display that included tulips submerged upside down in a water filled glass vase. That was juxtaposition for sure, but it worked, and was beautiful and unusual at the same time. A caterer once told me that he constantly comes up with new foods and presentations not so much because the clients demand it, but because he gets bored doing the same things over and over.

Train yourself to think differently as you go through your everyday life and soon you'll be looking at the world with new eyes.

For yourself

Your appearance and demeanor can be controlled - but only by you. Decide what you want to project to your clients and fellow vendors, and then follow it in all you do from the style of your attire to your business cards. This becomes your image. You can get help on it by reading books, or asking friends for their input. See prior sections of this book for a further discussion on image building and branding.

Nuances

An important part of being a top wedding vendor is being aware of nuances – those small distinctions between things. This is what sets a great vendor apart from a good one. This is where it can really show that you "understand" and another person doesn't. This extends beyond your work to life in general, in fact.

Nuances are the subtleties that distinguish the good from the great, the pretty from beautiful, the average from the exceptional, ad infinitum. It is here where you find the subtle variations in such lofty pursuits as classical music, in fine food and wines, in artistic endeavors and in such mundane things as personal grooming, in manners, in conduct of business.

Those who are aware of and understand and appreciate nuances are ahead of the game in both business and life. This doesn't mean they are snobbish or better than others and should lord their extra knowledge or perceptions over others. It means they use that knowledge and those perceptions in carrying out their work (and life in general) on a higher plane that produces higher results for themselves and their clients alike.

The more you are exposed to different kinds of things the more you can learn to appreciate nuances. It is important that you look for the subtle differences in everything from clothing design and construction, to service in stores, hotels and restaurants, to the taste and presentation of wines and foods and on and on, and to expect more from persons or companies who provide whatever it is you're buying. Your high-end clients are often highly educated people who might also be well traveled. They will likely know or have been exposed to the differences and it behooves you to know as well. This is one way for you to even the playing field and you can learn much on your own by observation and self-study if necessary.

Ironclad Rule # 13: **It is your client's wedding, not yours.**

Designing a wedding

The first thing you must do in designing a wedding for a client is to determine what that client wants. What is their vision for their wedding? What memory do they want their guests to walk away with? Without this information the wedding could be just another cookie cutter wedding that blends in with all the others.

So how do you find out the client's vision? Ask them. It might be via an extensive interview along with a questionnaire you have prepared that asks things such as their favorite foods, music, fabrics and colors. Ask them to collect pictures from magazines and books that they like, even if it's one flower or a small element. Get a feel for their style.

> I sometimes think that a marriage counselor would have fun with some of the couples and the way they answer the questions. I've had one or two brides who flatly stated that the groom's opinions didn't matter and would not be considered in the wedding plans.

Determine what elements of the wedding are most important to them by having both the bride and groom give a priority rank to each element of the wedding. I use a form for this that has a column for the bride, one for the groom, and one for the compromise rank when they can't agree.

The concept for the form I use came from Sharon Jansen of Special Event Business Advisors (SEBA) and I thank her for the inspiration. Please see the appendix for a copy of the form.

Before beginning to design a wedding it is imperative that you know what your client can and will spend. Just asking them what they want to spend might not garner the information you need. Some clients will hedge saying they just want it nice, or that it doesn't matter. But all brides want a nice wedding and it does matter to most what the cost is. Some are reticent to give a number thinking you will think it's too low. Or they might feel that if they say a number you'll raise your price to get that amount without delivering value not realizing that a reputable vendor would not think of doing that.

So I ask them for the dollar amount they don't want to go above. Some will answer straightaway with a figure; others will need a little coaxing so I gently say "how about X dollars?" I usually start on the high side of where I think they'd be comfortable and watch their body language or listen to their voice if it's a phone conversation. If they grimace or gasp I work downward. Occasionally they'll go upward and eventually we arrive at a number. It's immaterial what that number is. It's only important that both you and the client feel comfortable with it and that it's a reasonable number to achieve the type of wedding they desire and you can produce.

If you are the wedding planner you will need to cover the entire wedding in your cost breakdown and it is hoped that you will have been hired before too many other vendors to make sure that the contracts already signed are in line with reality. I've found that it is more accurate to think of the total cost of the wedding in terms of how much it costs per guest. A couple that comes in with $50,000 and 50 guests is going to get a far different wedding than the couple who comes in with $50,000 and 300 guests. The cost of certain elements of the wedding are fixed costs and will be the about the same no matter the number of guests. For example a photographer or videographer can be the same price for both a larger wedding and a smaller one, as can the music. Flowers and décor will vary with the number of tables and certainly food and beverages will as well.

Once the financial parameters are established, as the planner you must then prepare a comprehensive financial worksheet. I try not to use the word "budget" as it's just not a pretty word and sounds constricting rather than open and creative. I consider the financial worksheet a roadmap for the entire planning process and all my vendor recommendations are based upon the numbers therein. If you are a vendor who is responsible for just a portion of the wedding you must find out what your allotment of the total is and work with the client and the planner to stay in the proper range.

It's a good idea to have a form in your computer (possibly Excel) that you begin all estimates with and which can be easily updated for the changes, which can be many. Handwritten estimates presented to clients are inefficient and unprofessional and are not consistent with being a high end wedding vendor.

Of course, clients are free to change their financial parameters at any time - and often do - usually going upward instead of downward. Many times they see something they must have and, if they are in a position to dig a little deeper into the pocket, decide to spring for it.

Some vendors will prepare a proposal that reads like a wish list, itemizing everything the clients expressed an interest in during the initial interview. The clients can then choose those that are most important or appealing to them and line out the others. If you use this method your initial proposal will obviously be more than the amount allotted but you will eventually get to where the client wishes to be in both cost and style. You must be sure to let the client and planner know that you have purposely made the proposal high and that it can be adjusted to their needs, otherwise you risk frightening them off in the first read-through. You might show certain items as options after sub-totaling the basic ones. That way they can see two bottom lines with the smaller one perhaps being more palatable on the initial review. With experience you'll learn which way works best for you and your clients.

Be sure to add any sales tax to your initial proposal as it has to be part of the bottom line for a client working with a tight budget. I've seen clients disappointed that a proposal they thought was within their means suddenly became eight per cent more, putting a strain on the finances and looking like the vendor was trying to pull a fast one by upping the price once they agreed to the service. Most people do not want to increase their financial allotment by eight percent across the board and some simply cannot, so it's best to avoid that kind of surprise. The same principle goes for delivery, shipping or set up charges. Always deal with the bottom line costs.

Once you have determined the look of the wedding, and have a contract in place, you might want to set up a demonstration of all the decorative elements for the client to review or to make final decisions. If you are the wedding planner you will likely be in charge of arranging the demo. Naturally you don't set up the entire room but you use a section of the room to set up a table or two with different linens, chairs or dishes as the case may be, a centerpiece or two and the decorative lighting. Have the vendors arrive early to set up and bring your client in for the most dramatic presentation only after all is ready. You might even have appropriate background music on a portable CD player for the full effect.

A demonstration is especially important for a high-end wedding but it might not be cost effective for you or the vendors to go to such lengths for the average priced wedding. Keep in mind the time involved for such a presentation when you are pricing your services. You can scale the demo according to the price range of the wedding and if appropriate, can even have a food tasting at the same time.

Clients love this kind of presentation and it gives them a wonderful way to envision the room the way it will look on the wedding day. This is a time for refining all the design elements and making sure they exactly catch the clients' vision. This is also the "fun" part of the job that everyone thinks of when you say you are in the wedding business.

Part Three

Wedding Vendors by Discipline

With anecdotes, examples and quotes from established vendors

Following is an alphabetical listing of over 25 disciplines of vendors specific to the field of weddings. Each has an in depth discussion of the qualities and requirements which, when put into practice along with the above information, will practically guarantee success in the wedding business.

It is always important to strive to do the best you can at all times. If you are continuously trying to improve and grow your business, and I'm sure you are or you most likely wouldn't be reading this book, you can't help but have the success you are seeking.

Bakers

The wedding cake is an important focal point of the reception and should carry out the theme or style of the wedding. Some couples give more importance to the cake than others but, of course, all of them want it to taste good. Taste is a very personal thing so there is no single recipe for success in that respect. Many bakers develop their own very distinct style of decorating, or have a signature flavor, or might have a "secret" or family recipe, any of which can provide them with a marketing opportunity. Top bakers are very accommodating and flexible in the flavors they combine and the designs they'll do, but they also know their limitations and will not attempt something they don't believe is going to be perfect.

Design

Some brides have a clear vision of their cake from the moment they begin their wedding plans, and will even bring a magazine photo of a cake they would like you to copy, while others will need help with their decision.

For the latter, having nice photo albums (with at least some professional photos – not just snapshots) of prior cakes you have baked is important to illustrate to brides the type of work you are capable of as well as the venues where you have delivered your product. A collection of magazine photos that you have neatly organized into a loose-leaf binder is another aid for your sales, as are cake books and specialty journals that show myriad wedding cake ideas. You might offer to pick up a motif from her wedding gown design and incorporate it into the cake design.

Tastings

Offering tastings is an important part of your sales pitch. After all, how can anyone decide to order if they don't have an opportunity to taste the cake before ordering it? Virtually all bakers I know offer them, but how the tastings are conducted is what sets them apart and puts them into that field known as a "top wedding vendor". If several people are attending the tasting give them each a separate little plate and fork. If you are offering several flavors the pieces of cake you give them needn't be larger than a 2 inch square but to expect them to eat off the same plate is rude. For example if a bride comes in with her future mother in law it may make both of them uncomfortable to share a plate. The engaged couple, on the other hand, may even chose to use the same fork, but that's their option. Disposable plates, napkins and forks are certainly permissible but the presentation should be as gracious as a nice restaurant. Just as a top restaurant will not just toss a pile of forks and napkins on the table neither will a top baker. It's thoughtful to offer water, even in paper cups, as sweets can make the tasters thirsty.

> One of the most interesting cake tastings I ever attended was presented on a large flat board on which the baker had placed a slice of each of her cake flavors individually labeled and accompanied by rows of each of her frostings and fillings, also individually labeled. All who attended the tasting could "build their own" cake by mixing and matching the flavors on their own little plate. The bride described the cake she ordered as "the quintessential wedding cake" which any wedding cake baker would be complimented to hear, I'm sure. Perhaps part of that perception began at the tasting.

If you think having nice tastings costs you too much, raise your prices a bit to accommodate that. There are a few bakers who charge for the tasting then apply the cost of it to the cake if an order is placed. It will certainly screen out the less serious lookers but there is also a less gracious aspect to it that I feel cheapens the vendor somewhat. The prices I've encountered have been from $8 per person to $25 per flavor requested with the latter being a daunting amount in my experience. Because tastings are such an integral part of your selling mechanism, they should be considered part your marketing plan - both from a financial aspect and a time aspect.

From the time aspect, you can limit the days and times you meet with clients for tastings. That also puts you into a more exclusive area since you won't be considered a "cake mill" who offers tastings on demand. If you are aiming for the higher end market, you should pre-screen your clients anyway to make sure they can afford your prices.

A marketing hint: offer to send a sample of the bride's two favorite flavors home to whomever wasn't at the tasting but who might be instrumental in making the final decision – maybe the groom or the bride's dad. It's amazing how much they like being considered and the baker is then the topic of conversation for the rest of the day and at the dinner table. Package it up with your label on the container and even a box becomes a marketing tool! Just be sure you are not giving a perishable sample that's going to sit in a warm car and risk spoilage that will come back to haunt you.

Conduct the tastings at a roomy, uncluttered table with comfortable chairs. Many wedding cakes come from working bakeries that have a café, too. Trying to do business over the din can be distracting for both the prospective client and the salesperson so arrange your tastings during off hours or have a table as far from the center of noise as possible. Making the tastings as professional as possible will do much to enhance your image.

Delivery and set up

Many of the horror stories of weddings have to do with the cake. Maybe it's because there are lots of amateur bakers who think it's easy to bake a wedding cake and don't understand that they are often a feat of engineering.

Delivery of the cake to the reception must be timed between the set-up of the cake table and the guests' arrival. Be specific on when your cake is needed, then deliver it exactly when you say you are going to be there. When working at a venue you have not previously delivered to, make sure you inquire about the loading dock and the distance you'll have to go to the reception room.

Make sure your cake is not being placed in a sunny window or outdoors when it will be exposed to the sun or other elements. These questions must be asked when the cake is ordered and you must refuse to do a whipped cream frosting if there is even a modicum of possibility that your cake could spoil and cause illness to someone who eats it. Remember that wedding cakes are often cut many hours after delivery and food safety is a very important consideration. Even if spoilage wasn't a consideration, the sun could melt the cake causing it to slide or fall.

Top bakers are as particular about the presentation of their cake as they are the

One wedding cake, made by a professional, was placed on a table set up by the florist who apparently didn't know to lock the table legs. After an hour or so the table collapsed taking the cake with it. Fortunately this was before the guests were invited into the reception room and the caterer placed an immediate call to the baker for help. The baker made an emergency run, bringing two of the bakery's display cakes for the bride and groom to choose from as they posed for their cake cutting photos. He also brought several sheet cakes the bakery had in stock which were served from the kitchen. He saved the day and the guests didn't even know what had happened.

design. Using fresh flowers on cakes is a popular trend and you could find the florist destroying the design of the cake by the way they place the flowers on it. Top bakers contact the florist in advance and order the matching flowers which they then place on the cake at setup.

Always be sure to bring along some extra frosting and anything else you might need to patch up any minor mishaps that might occur during transport and set up.

Bands

There is an ongoing discussion of which is better for a wedding reception - a band or DJ. There is no conclusive answer to this question and this book will not attempt to resolve it. It's a little like the chicken or egg question. Bands tend to be a bigger production and can bring a more formal feel, while a DJ has a wider range of selections available with the original artists and will generally be less costly. The bride and groom will ultimately decide the look and feel they want for the reception then choose what's best for their needs.

Requirements

Be sure to let the wedding planner or venue know in advance the size of riser or stage your group requires as well as the number of dedicated circuits you will need for your equipment. Visit the venue in advance if you have not worked there before to make sure you know how to access the loading dock and the room in which you will be performing. At the very least telephone the planner or venue about it. If you require a green room with soft drinks or food, or a place to stow your equipment, be sure to spell that out in advance via your contract as well.

Master of ceremonies

No matter who writes the timeline for the reception, the person on the microphone controls the flow of the reception and must have a full understanding of the flow AND be willing to work with the planner who has made the timeline. A poor or uncooperative master of ceremonies (MC) can ruin a reception by throwing the timing off. And it is arrogant not to consider the other vendors and their needs. An example of this is having guests up and dancing when the food is ready for service. This causes havoc in the kitchen and can result in a cold or overcooked meal, something no chef or banquet captain ever wants to see and certainly no clients wants to pay for.

A full dance floor all night is not the mark of a successful party as is sometimes mistakenly believed. Rather a successful party has various moods, each appropriate to what is taking place, and the music should be matched to the activity such as quiet music for dining and conversation, then more upbeat music for the party.

A wedding reception is not the same as a nightclub gig in any way, shape or form. Club musicians often can play wonderful music but, unless the band member acting as MC understands and respects how a reception works, it can be a real disaster.

An MC must know how to control a crowd without being demanding, sarcastic or begging. He or she must have stage presence and a good speaking voice but keep the spoken words to a minimum. The MC must leave his ego at home. This is not about him, it is about giving the guests and bride and groom a great reception and working as part of the team.

Demos

Prospective clients often will ask to hear or see a band before hiring it, which is understandable. Many bands have a demo videotape to show or send to prospective clients, or do so by way of a wedding planner. There are two sides to that coin, the first being that it allows the couple to get a feel for what the band does on stage, how they interact and how they look. The opposite side of the coin is that sometimes the clients are so busy looking at the gown the lead singer is wearing, or they don't like the song that's on the demo video, or some other things that distract them, that they forget to listen to the quality of the musicians, which is the whole point of a demo in the first place.

The demo video had better be good as well as current or it will lose business for you. Make sure it is professionally done and really shows your band the way you want to be shown. Having no demo is better than a poor one. I am not a fan of demo videos made in a studio as they lack the energy of a performance before an audience and often have a stilted quality, or poor lighting or no stage. It seems that every performer is better playing to a real audience where the energy flows both ways.

Editing clips from real performances into a demo video can be effective if done right. Here's where relationship building comes in handy as you can ask videographers you've worked with at prior weddings for permission to use their work. Or you can arrange in advance of a reception to have them shoot some footage of the band specifically for that purpose.

As an alternative to a video some bands have their demos on CD (cassette tapes are pretty outdated by now) which allows the prospective client to hear the music without being distracted by visual images as mentioned above. There is still a danger of the listener judging the performance by the song that's being featured rather than the actual quality of the music, but that is less of an issue than with a visual.

Ironclad Rule #14 - <u>Never</u> invite prospective clients to another event.

Inviting prospective clients to a gig

Some bands or agencies actually invite a prospective client to hear the band at another reception they are playing.

> A bride once told me that when she was looking for a band, a booking agency I had never heard of got her and her fiancé into a private party to see and hear a band they were considering. My thought was, if they hire this band how many strangers are going to be invited to their wedding to hear the band perform?

No matter how much you want the job it is <u>not</u> professional behavior and should not be suggested. If requested you must explain to the bride and groom that you would not invite a stranger to their reception and thus would not take them to a stranger's reception. A private party is not your sales tool. It is just that - a <u>private</u> party.

Behavior at reception

Band members hired for a wedding reception are NOT invited guests. They are working and should individually and collectively behave as such. This means they do not fraternize with guests. They go to a specifically designated area for their breaks and eat the vendor meal which is provided in an area out of sight of the guests. They, as all vendors, are here to work, not to join the party.

Ironclad rule #6 (repeated) – The band members never, repeat <u>never</u>, go to the bar and order a drink.

Eating and drinking at reception

The band members NEVER drink alcohol at a gig no matter how much more "creative" they claim it makes them and they do not go through the buffet line unless that is the advance arrangement for the vendor meal. In that case they go through discreetly after all guests have been through then go eat at the designated location behind the scenes.

Ironclad Rule #7 (repeated) The band members do not eat passed or displayed hors d'oeuvres.

They are not guests and should not act as guests.

If a guest sends them over a drink they graciously thank the guest but do not touch the drink. It doesn't matter if it's the groom or father of the bride who sends the drink. A band must maintain its professional standards at all times or risk not being referred by the planner or venue again or worse, have something happen that could be blamed on their consumption of alcohol and suffer some severe consequences.

Bringing groupies or relatives

Musicians on a wedding reception job are not to invite their "groupies" or friends or family members to accompany them to the reception or invite them to come by later. It is simply not consistent with being a top wedding band.

This is a paid job and unless it's "Bring Your Family and Friends to Work" day they should be nowhere near the job - even on New Year's Eve!

Ironclad Rule #15: Appropriate music must be playing when the doors are formally opened for the guests.

Adding overtime

Occasionally a wedding couple will want to extend the music on the spot as the wedding reception is going full speed ahead at the designated finish time. Top bands will have already discussed this eventuality so the clients knows how much it will cost them, how that payment will be collected and if, indeed, it will even be possible due to prior commitments of the musicians and/or the venue. If you have a credit card on file and think the possibility of extending the time is a good one, you can ask the client in advance to sign an authorization for the extra service. Let them know you will destroy the form if it's not used. Or you can have such a form with you at the reception and ask them to sign it as soon as you agree to extend. You could also ask for cash which may not be readily available unless you make them fully aware in advance that this is the only way you'll agree to the extension. Or you could take a personal check, which could be risky. Or you could bill them later, which could be even more risky. Make a policy for this and be consistent with it or you could be burned and end up paying your band members out of your pocket for the extra time.

As a rule, however, extending the party is not generally a good idea. Well planned wedding receptions wind down naturally and people begin to leave after several hours. I always recommend leaving with the guests wanting more. While there is usually a hard core group of party people on the dance floor who would dance into the wee hours, it is not necessary to extend the party just for them. They are often intoxicated and would dance like robots as long as there is music. Proper selection of the music in the final set can do much to end the party in the right mood and a skillful band will do this.

Many couples believe that their guests will stay a very long time at their reception and want it to end in the wee hours which I tend to discourage as the bulk of their guests will leave within about five hours of arrival. During the planning stages I ask them when the last time was that they stayed at someone's party over six hours and they often understand my point. On a wedding day the guests (and the wedding party as well) will have been getting ready, making their way to the wedding, attending the wedding, then the cocktail hour, then the reception and then making their way home. That is a huge time investment for them and most will be ready to leave before the last note is played. There must be some reason that most hotels and other venues offer a six hour time frame for the wedding and reception.

Royalties

As a band leader it is your responsibility to know the laws pertaining to royalties and the payment of same. Check with your legal advisor to see how the use of another's intellectual property affects your business.

Barbara Wallace

Please read the section entitled "Disk Jockeys" for further
information.

Bartenders and beverage providers

All bartenders and persons dispensing alcoholic beverages must be highly insured and licensed by the proper governing body in the area they will be performing their duties. Only very responsible persons should tend bar because of the strict laws that govern liquor liability in most states. For example anyone appearing to be intoxicated must not be served and it is the responsibility of the bartender to watch that. It is never acceptable for an unlicensed or uninsured person or group to serve alcoholic beverages.

It is imperative that you become familiar with the liquor laws in your state and strictly comply with them. There is far too much liability involved to leave this to chance.

Ironclad Rule #16: <u>Never</u> place a tip jar or cup on the bar at a private function.

Tip jar

It is very tacky to expect the guests to feed the jar and cheapens the event. (I think they are tacky in a retail food service store, too as it looks more like a begging bowl to me, but I'm swimming upstream on that one, I'm sure.) If a tip is offered, discreetly acknowledge it, and then place it in a jar that is out of sight – way out of sight. A host is paying for the bartending service and most are mortified at the thought of even intimating that their guests should pay anything while at their party.

Presentation

Having an attractively presented bar is just as important as having a nicely-presented buffet. Top bartending services or caterers coordinate their set up to reflect the theme of the event all the way down to the attire of the bartenders.

Be sure there are enough bars and bartenders to accommodate the number of guests, especially at the beginning of the cocktail hour. The first ten minutes of the cocktail hour that follows a ceremony are going to tax the bar the most because all guests have the same idea- that of getting their first drink.

At a special event of about 100 people there was one bar with a very slow bartender. Even though it was just the beginning of the cocktail hour the bar had not been not well stocked and he had already run out of certain wines and soft drinks. His attitude, facial expressions and demeanor were negative causing the guests waiting in line to grumble about it. His movement was very deliberate- he placed the cork back into the wine bottle after each pour and generally missed the point about speedy, cheerful service. This did not make a good impression especially at the start of the festivities.

Having some tray-passed white wine, champagne, sparkling water or a specialty drink will relieve that initial crush at the bar while giving an air of elegance to the event. A rule of thumb is to have a bar and bartender for each 100 guests. But that could vary depending on the speed and experience of the bartender and the complexity of the drinks being mixed. For example, pouring a glass of wine takes less time than shaking a martini which takes far less time than blending specialty margaritas.

Nothing can disgruntle guests more than having to line up and wait for drinks or food and their general perception is that they are waiting much longer than they actually are. If they don't let you know it right then, they will at the least walk away with a negative impression and will probably tell all their friends and associates.

Serving minors and those who are obviously intoxicated

This is important not only from a social standpoint but it is more important from a legal standpoint. The host and the bartenders could be liable for any problems that arise from either minors or obviously intoxicated persons being served alcohol, especially if they drive. It is up to you to have a policy in place in advance on how to handle such occurrences and then enforce it unfailingly.

Calligraphers

Calligraphy is an important part of the wedding industry as it's often the first thing a guest sees when they receive a wedding invitation and will carry through to the reception with place cards and menus. Talent, neatness and promptness are the three most important qualities of a calligrapher. Top calligraphers have samples of their work readily available to send to prospective clients either by fax or mail that clearly state the name of the hand(s) [sometimes incorrectly called "fonts"] they offer. It's important to show all letters of the alphabet in both upper and lower case so the client can easily see them and not have to try to imagine them. A fully addressed envelope mailed to a prospective client is an excellent illustration.

You must make clear to the client how you will accept the master list from which the writing is taken and then make sure the client understands that such list must be letter perfect especially if the list contains long and/or foreign names. All titles such as Dr., Ms., Miss., The Honorable, etc. must be clear. You must explain to the client that you will simply write what you see and that it is not your job to correct mistakes or edit the list. As a courtesy the client should note any unusual spellings of common names just to avoid confusion.

A list of fees that is given out with the samples is important, too. A bride and groom have little if any idea of what the cost of this service might be and are often muddled at the idea of inner and outer envelopes and such terms as "envelope set" so the more information they get the easier they will be to work with.

You must carefully proofread your finished work prior to returning it to the client. It is far easier to catch errors at that point than to have an envelope or two returned piecemeal by the client for correction. The fewer errors seen by the client, the higher your reputation as a calligrapher stays.

Many things having to do with weddings seem to be last minute and the calligraphy is no exception. In fact, place cards are a prime example because the bride either forgets she'll need them until then or has many last minute changes as her final guest list changes almost hourly.

There are several ways to assign tables and the final choice has to do with how much last minute work the bride is prepared to do. You must be able to explain the pros and cons of each method as follows: A couple who wishes to assign a specific seat at the table for each guest is in for more last minute work than a couple who simply assigns a table to a group of guests who then choose the particular seat at that table when they enter the reception room.

The former needs two forms of seating information. One outside the dining room to convey to the guest the number of the table at which they are to sit and a second form at the table to convey to them which specific seat they are to take. The information outside the dining room can be either on a decorative, possibly framed, master list in alphabetical order which is large enough to be easily read from several feet away or a card bearing the table number that is inside a small envelope bearing the guest's name(s).

The card in envelope style is known as a table card (sometimes the term "escort card" is used but that is actually a misnomer) and can be a very easy way to handle last minutes changes as the table number cards inside are interchangeable. If the calligrapher makes a full set of table number cards for each table (one for each possible seat at the table) and a name envelope for each possible attendee or couple any last minute changes are taken care of by simply moving the table number from envelope to envelope.

The cards placed on the table at the specific seat bear the guest's name only, with the possible addition of a symbol signifying the entrée choice, and can be moved around at will as well while a decorative master list must be fully redone if there are guest name additions.

If the uncertainty of the final count draws into the final week before the wedding, I often suggest making a place card for any guest whose attendance might be even a remote possibility, and then discarding that place card if they aren't able to attend. It saves stress at the last minute on both the bride and the calligrapher and costs comparatively little.

Caterers

Caterers come in all styles from the smallest single person operation to a large commercial organization capable of serving over a thousand meals at one event. Whichever you are, your business must be conducted as professionally as any other wedding vendor – maybe even more so because your costs will take up as much as half of the wedding budget which in some cases will be in the tens of thousands of dollars. The couple has to feel comfortable with this kind of expenditure.

Most wedding clients are not used to putting on big parties and have no idea how much a dinner for a hundred or more people might cost. They often forget to consider the cost of service, the rentals or the tax and service charge, and are shocked to see the total in the end. Even those that dine out often sometimes don't relate the food costs at their wedding to that of a good restaurant.

A top caterer takes the opportunity to educate the client at the outset and gives a clear, itemized proposal so they will understand exactly what to expect in the planning stage, during the event and after the event is over.

For example, questions to answer are: Will they get to taste the food? How many service staff will you provide? What will become of the food at the end of the event? Will your staff be the last ones out? How do you handle vendor meals?

Tastings

A huge question when a client is considering a caterer is what does the food taste like and how it will be presented. These are very important considerations and offering a food tasting answers both. The question is: does the tasting take place before or after the client books? Some caterers will only do it after they secure the booking with a large deposit, others charge for tastings if done before the contract is made, some do them complimentary as a marketing tool at the first meeting and others don't do them at all.

As a wedding planner I have found that those who offer tastings prior to the booking have more success than those who are reticent to take the time to "strut their stuff" if they don't have a deposit. One of the most well known caterers in my area who is busy with multiple high-end events almost every weekend invites the prospective clients and the planner into his office adjacent to his kitchen. He sits everyone down to a nicely set table and proceeds to serve an array of beautifully presented dishes that demonstrate his chef's talent and style. Few of the clients walk away without booking him right there. He feels it's a great form of advertising and is worth the time and money to effectuate it. The planner doesn't usually partake of the tasting but some caterers insist, which is another way of marketing to the person who can bring in additional clients.

A small caterer or one just starting out might find it too burdensome, both financially and physically, to host tastings prior to booking, and that is understandable. (I suppose a person posing as a client could make a career out of going from caterer to caterer and eating "free food".) However it is acceptable to charge the client for a tasting – not for profit but to cover the expense - and I think most clients would understand. You might tell them that you'll apply the charge as a credit to final bill if they do end up booking your company. It doesn't have to be full meal for each participant. In fact it's best not to overfeed the prospective client and merely let them have samples of many of your offerings.

Some caterers have a designated evening each month where prospective clients are invited for a tasting and others have a restaurant or other retail food service facility where the prospective client can taste and see the presentation of the food.

Of course, you can get catering jobs without offering tastings at all, but you'll have to be a very good sales person and/or have some strong referrals from planners and others who can vouch for your quality and expertise.

> I once had a fairly young bridal couple meeting with a caterer and the caterer brought a pretty box of homemade chocolate chip cookies to the initial meeting. The groom was sold at that moment and the job was sealed.

A very nice but relatively inexpensive marketing tool, if you don't or can't offer tastings, is to bring along a sample of one of your specialties to the initial client meeting. Having a plate of homemade scones presented in a beautifully wrapped package can do wonders to set the mood and give the prospective client a little sneak preview of your creativity and presentation. Or, imagine being the client and being presented with a couple of fancy chocolate dipped strawberries as a gift from the prospective caterer. I think most people would agree that that makes a pretty good impression.

If you're hosting the meeting in your office some simple beverages should be available. Just remember to let them know what business you're in and make the presentation commensurate with the impression you want them to take away from the meeting. Use every opportunity you have to promote your image.

Ironclad Rule #17: Do <u>not</u> invite a prospective client to another client's party to see the set up or taste the food.

Inviting prospective clients to another event

This is not consistent with being a top wedding vendor. You are not the host of the party and therefore have no authority to invite people, either on your own or by asking the current client for permission. Occasionally a prospective client will ask to come by before the guests arrive, but even this is sketchy as it's your busiest time and you should be focusing on the event rather than selling to another client. The full set up won't likely be in place anyway.

Here's where a great portfolio comes in to illustrate your set up. If you want that prospective client to taste the food you're serving, consider making an extra portion or two and arranging a way to deliver it to him, or invite him in to your place of business to sample it when it's fresh. This is the kind of creative thinking that will earn you some points.

Be prepared on the event day

Naturally a highly trained staff is of utmost importance - each with assigned duties that will be carried out professionally. As they interact with your client, their guests and the other vendors each of them is representing you and will thus reflect on your reputation.

It's a good idea to have a decent amount of extra cash with you so

At one off premise event site the custom made linens were delivered in time for set up. However, they were covered with lint from the manufacturing process so we dispatched a runner to the nearest store to purchase several lint rollers and called in a few emergency staff to roll all the cloths.

that if an emergency arises- such as if you run out of something important or you have the need for something you did not foresee - you can dispatch one of your staff to the nearest store to purchase it.

Presentation

It is said that we eat with our eyes first so certainly a beautiful presentation can enhance the enjoyment of our food. If you are a better cook than a display artist find someone who can assist you with conceiving a great display presentation during the planning process and have them on site to help you build it during set up of the event. It doesn't have to be a huge project with a multitude of props but it will take some forethought so be prepared with the proper risers and extra linens for example.

Look at magazines for ideas and the latest trends in food presentation. Notice how props can be used to enhance the theme of the event and, if there is no theme, discuss with your client how even a simple one might be incorporated. Obviously, decorations should not be gaudy or distract from the food but merely setting out a row of chafing dishes on a flat table leaves much to be desired.

Portfolio and photos

A caterer is one of the wedding vendors who most needs a portfolio and the more impressive it is, the easier it is to sell your services. Please refer to the prior section of this book that discusses a wedding vendor's portfolio. You can't expect a client to trust you with verbal descriptions for both the food and the presentation - it's too much of a stretch for most people, especially those who are not used to giving parties. They must get a visual on it, so increase your chances of getting the sales by having as much to show as you can. Hire your own photographer if you must to get the photos you need and want for your portfolio.

Catering Managers at venues

Catering managers at wedding venues often have the title "Wedding Coordinator" which is somewhat misleading. It implies that the manager will act as the coordinator of the entire wedding, which is generally not accurate. Most catering managers focus on the food and beverage and set up of the venue, then depart from the reception once the meal has begun. They typically do not handle the myriad of personal services to the bride that is expected of a professional wedding consultant, coordinator or planner as such details are well beyond the scope of their duties.

Some venues have a catering sales manager who specializes in showing and booking the venue for prospective clients. The active file is then transferred to a service manager (who might be called a" catering manager", a "wedding coordinator" or perhaps an "event coordinator"). At other venues, one person performs both functions.

There are some venues, usually large hotels, which require that a wedding client hire an outside professional wedding coordinator to assist them with the rehearsal and ceremony thus relieving the catering manager or the staff of having to mind the details on the wedding day.

Top catering managers work closely with the outside wedding coordinator to make sure the details are attended to and wisely welcome the assistance, as a good outside coordinator will handle them with ease and accuracy. Both are members of the same team and working for the bridal couple, and it is important to work toward the common goal of making the wedding a great day for the bride and groom.

Most venues have a set of rules in place to ensure the smooth flow of an event, and as the catering manager it is your responsibility to convey and enforce them relative to all vendors who will work on the property. If these rules are reasonable and, even if in a vendor's opinion they are not, they must abide by them (remember a top vendor is a team player). To be a top catering manager you should approach all relationships with vendors and clients in a positive, non-confrontational manner and take the time to review the requirements so the vendor can embrace them. You can be "in charge" without taking on a bossy or drill sergeant attitude and, in fact, will get farther with a pleasant attitude than the opposite. Civility and a cool temperament are always in style and are extra important during a tense situation.

Of course, there are vendors who are not as professional as you would like and then your job becomes one of education. If a vendor is not of the caliber that meets the venue's expectations you do not have to refer them in the future. Here again is an illustration of a vendor's behavior making or breaking him.

Own recommendations

Many venues have a preferred vendor list which they share with prospective clients. Some require that vendors on the list be used - sometimes because the venue or catering manager is taking a percentage of the vendor's fee. This is not an acceptable practice and does a disservice to the client since most brides are planning a wedding for the one and only time in their life and know very little about how to achieve the best result. The best result for that bride isn't necessarily using your venue's required or preferred vendors.

Naturally a vendor who has worked at a particular site is more familiar with it, but you can assist a vendor who is working there for the first time if he is willing to work as part of the team. It is hoped that they will contact you well in advance of the wedding day and a site visit might even be arranged. But, of course, if you have to educate new vendors constantly it becomes a bit of a burden and it's clear why you prefer to refer those you know.

Sometimes the preferred vendor list is a paid listing. By requiring a vendor to pay to be on the preferred vendor list your venue is going into murky waters. The vendor then has a right to be referred by the venue, and your catering department is obligated to refer him, putting you in the position of not being able to remove the vendor from your list if they do not perform to consistently high standards. It is certainly not an objective listing, but the clients generally do not know that. I see this actually as a disservice to the client.

An unpaid listing puts your venue in control and allows you to remove the vendor's name anytime you wish and for any reason you wish. It also is fairer to the clients who are then getting a less biased recommendation.

Naturally you have your favorites as some vendors just stand out and are consistently easier to work with. This is the kind of word of mouth referrals that are invaluable to a vendor and these are the kind of relationships to cultivate. If the client has an outside wedding planner who is hired to perform full service wedding planning for a bride and groom, it is not your place to refer the vendors as the wedding planner might have good reasons for recommending particular vendors to their client. Everyone must have respect for the other's position. Remember, it is a team.

As wedding coordinator

If your job of catering manager is truly that of the coordinator of the entire wedding, and the wedding couple is on board with that, you must undertake your duties with as much seriousness and professionalism as possible. All phases of the wedding, which includes pre-planning such as advice on many miscellaneous issues such as invitations and arranging for limousines, etc., must be handled for the bride and groom and they must expect to pay the going rate for the service. To hold oneself out as a full service planner entails all this and much more and it's the rare catering manager who has enough time to handle her in-house duties and take on full service brides as well.

A wedding consultant colleague of mine related her treatment by a catering manager in a mid-range hotel as very rude and unprofessional. On the wedding day my colleague was snubbed and whispered about within ear range as she tried to go about the duties the bride and groom hired her for. The regular vendors "referred" by the hotel were a part of the shunning and generally made a very unpleasant experience. My colleague actually was hired by the bride and her mother because they were having such a difficult time with the catering manager themselves and refused to deal directly with her as the wedding approached. Her behavior certainly proved them right.

For everyone's peace of mind, full service wedding planning is better left to a full time wedding planner.

Though an extreme example, the above illustrates how difficult things can be. To be fair, it must be pointed out that most catering managers welcome the assistance of a good outside coordinator as it makes their job far easier. Top venues rely on them, in fact.

Churches and Church Wedding Directors

Churches generally have a person, sometimes a volunteer, who handles the weddings at the site. That person is generally known as a wedding director or coordinator but handles the wedding coordinating only as it relates to the church, such as directing the rehearsal and the actual ceremony and enforcing the church rules. Some churches do many weddings and make a considerable income from the fees, and, in fact, have a very short time frame between the ceremonies, making it important to begin exactly on time.

If the bridal couple has hired an outside wedding coordinator she must be especially careful not to infringe on the church wedding director's position and should not give her opinions or try to circumvent the rules. She should make it clear that she is there to observe and assist only if necessary and invited by the church person in charge. The church rules are in place either to protect the church property and/or to observe the religious code and must be respected by all participants of the bridal party.

On the other hand, as a top church wedding director you should always be gracious and should practice the tenets of the religion you are representing by conducting yourself in an exemplary manner. You can establish your "in charge" position from the beginning of the relationship with the bride and groom, not with bossiness but with clarity of purpose, graciousness and firmness, if necessary.

It is important to conduct yourself professionally even if you are volunteering or making just a small stipend for each wedding. Your duty to return telephone calls is just as important as any other wedding vendor's. This position should be treated as a job rather than a hobby.

Rules and enforcement of them

Almost all churches have strict rules about what can and cannot be done, either on the premises or as part of the wedding service itself. It is very important that any wedding vendor who will be working at the church, either prior to or during the ceremony, be 100 percent familiar with the rules in advance. This includes what kinds of flowers and/or decor, if any, are allowed; if videography is allowed and how the camera(s) can be used; if or where photography is allowed before, during and after the ceremony and if there are any clothing restrictions or requirements. Please review the section on appearance and dress for an in depth discussion.

Rehearsals

Almost all wedding ceremonies require a rehearsal and this is one of the most important duties of your job as the church wedding director. It is extremely important that all details be discussed with the wedding couple in advance so they can be rehearsed during the rehearsal, not endlessly discussed as the other participants lose interest and begin to talk among themselves. Having a rehearsal last more than an hour (many can be conducted in 45 minutes) is hard on the participants, especially if the group is large and not of the religious persuasion of the bride and groom.

Stories abound at the treatment of outside wedding coordinators by church wedding directors. Once I encountered one who actually ignored me as if I was invisible during the whole process even though the bride invited (and paid for) me to be there for the rehearsal and the ceremony and well as the rest of the wedding day. I had called the church lady in advance to tell her that I was there to assist the bride as she got ready and that I had no intention of butting in to the way she conducted the processional and ceremony. She obviously felt so threatened by my presence that she couldn't even be civil and actually wouldn't even answer me when I addressed her.

Working from a written format is important and will contain the names of all the wedding party members, the order in which they will enter, and by whom they are to be escorted. It will also detail their places at the altar and their duties during the ceremony such as holding the bride's bouquet, carrying the rings, reading a passage, etc. It will include the names of the musical selections and when and how long they will be played. You and the bridal couple must prepare it in advance.

Start the rehearsal by asking all participants to be seated. Welcome them and state your name and title in a clear voice loud enough for all to hear and to establish your position as being in charge. You might offer a prayer to settle the crowd and establish the mood as one of seriousness. If the officiant is there you will introduce him or her. Discuss the church rules so there is no confusion as to what is or isn't allowed before, during or after the ceremony. Give a brief verbal discussion of what will occur, and then ask all participants to take their place at the altar as if they had just entered from the procession.

Run through the ceremony quickly, not reading every word, but hitting the highlights or places where some action will be taken of which the participants must be aware. Then practice the recessional. Briefly discuss any questions or minor changes, and then run through the entire ceremony again from the top, including the protocol seating. If there is any confusion the whole thing can be practiced again but this is generally not necessary. Introducing the bride's outside wedding planner and letting her have a few minutes at the end of the rehearsal is a very considerate thing to do. This might be the first time the wedding party has met her and she can give them some brief instructions of what is going to happen during the reception and the rest of the wedding day. Keep in mind, she doesn't want to usurp your job and, like you, is simply trying to make the wedding day run as smoothly and efficiently as possible.

It might be helpful to also read the information entitled "Officiants" below.

Coordinators/consultants/planners

The terms wedding coordinator, wedding consultant and wedding planner are used interchangeably and while there is probably a slight difference in each term, all are acceptable ways to describe the same job and distinction will not be made between the terms and, in fact, they will be used interchangeably here.

At some level the idea of being a wedding coordinator is glamorous – perhaps because of several popular movies. The perception is that it's "fun" because everything is pretty and it's a happy day for the couple and their families and friends. As the coordinator you have to work very hard, often for months, to make the "fun" happen and none of the movies show those months plus the nine to fourteen hours you're on your feet the day of the wedding, or the last minute changes the bride's mom is making to the seating arrangements ten minutes before the reception is about to begin.

You are the person in charge of pulling all phases of the wedding plans together to make the wedding day run smoothly and are expected to be aware of everything having to do with the day. You must also be prepared to immediately solve any and all emergencies that might arise.

You will prepare and direct the timeline for the wedding day and all other vendors should be prepared to take direction from you. Make a very detailed timeline which includes the arrival and departure of every vendor. When preparing the timeline you must mentally walk through it to make sure that all times make sense. For example, you must be sure to give the limousine time to return from a drop off to another pickup if it is shuttling people. Or you must consider how long it will take to move a crowd into the banquet room from the cocktail reception as they don't just time warp to their tables when the dinner chimes are sounded A crowd of over 300 can take as long as 30 minutes to settle into their seats and not considering that can set your timeline back considerably.

The final written timeline is distributed no later than the beginning of the week of the wedding to all pertinent parties, along with maps to the venue and other information they must know, such as how to use the loading dock, where they will store their equipment, which rest rooms to use, where they will eat their vendor meal and the like. A note on the word "timeline": I use that term instead of "schedule" as the latter connotes that something will happen no matter what - as a bus will continue on its route whether or not passengers are there to board it.

The timeline must have some fluidity as the day progresses but serves as a check point and the skilled planner watches it closely to make sure the flow is reasonably on track. In fact, I carry my timeline folded in my suit pocket and consult it frequently. I make notes on it when each activity takes place and check it off. I don't rely on my memory to do anything, even if I do it at every wedding. Distractions constantly arise and it's safer to have everything written down. I also do not carry a clipboard, preferring to have both hands free. Plus I think it looks officious and laying it down someplace and forgetting it could cause guests to see "back of the house" information that they should not know about.

It is very important that you be highly organized and conduct yourself and your business in the most professional manner possible, as you will have to deal with all issues and problems that arise on the wedding day. You will be called upon to make instant decisions that will affect the outcome of the day and many of these decisions will be highly visible or sensitive.

You must be in control without trying to control everything. Bossiness and ordering people around are <u>not</u> the traits of a top wedding planner. You must remain calm and courteous even while being firm if the need for that arises. Your attitude will set the mood for the manner in which all other vendors and the wedding party will behave. The old adage "never let them see you sweat" is very important for a top wedding coordinator. You might be seething inside but externally are smiling and calm while solving the problems of the day.

Ironclad Rule #18: NEVER run or become agitated especially in the presence of the guests or bridal party.

Even behind the scenes the coordinator must stay calm and courteous. Remember, the vendors you work with will affect your reputation either good or bad. You might not think about it, but the serving staff and house men will observe you and they all talk. They see many weddings and events and know who does a great job.

To communicate with your assistants you might use walkie-talkies (preferably with an ear piece) so you are in constant communication with them especially in a venue that is very large, such as an estate or large hotel. Use them discreetly but be aware that they can be invaluable by saving you time and many steps. For large off-premise events the entire staff from valets to the caterers can be connected with walkie-talkies which can be rented along with their recharging system. The planner can then seem to be in more than one place at a time while remaining in a central position to direct the flow of the event from set up to strike.

Most wedding consultants have several levels of service and might do as little as assisting with the rehearsal and the wedding day, often referred to as "day of" wedding coordinating, a term I do not endorse at all.

No matter which kind of service is being performed, you are the liaison between the bride and all the vendors on the wedding day. Your goal should be to know so much that you do not have to bother the bride or her mother with details and questions that may arise on the wedding day. After all, they hired you to make the day easier for them and it should be.

> Offering "day of" service is not optimal in my mind as it's very difficult to really know what's going on without being involved in the wedding planning process for longer than the last few days. I wish wedding magazines would stop suggesting that brides hire someone "for at least the day of the wedding" One high-end catering manager likens hiring a 'day of' coordinator to the bride choosing her maid of honor the day before the wedding.

On the wedding day the key people who make the wedding and reception flow smoothly are the wedding coordinator, the banquet captain (who is in charge of the banquet staff and all food service) and the master of ceremonies (whether the band leader or a DJ) as they are the people who affect the timing of the event and good timing is what will make it memorable. They must be consulted before each activity takes place to ensure that it's timely. For example, the toasts cannot be introduced until the champagne is poured, and the serving staff must be free to do that, so the captain must be consulted prior to taking that step. The MC must be aware of when the food is ready to be served as the guests must be seated to receive their meal, and if they are up and dancing vigorously they will delay the service with the possible consequence of ruining the food.

The best wedding coordinators have many life experiences as they are called upon to advise their clients on etiquette, food and wine, design and style relating to textiles and flowers, psychology and much more. No one thinks to tell you you'll need to be a public speaker but what are you doing when you direct a wedding rehearsal? There might be as many as 30 people (who are only half listening) to organize and impart important information to in an orderly manner and in less than an hour.

Ironclad Rule #19: NEVER promise what you cannot deliver.

You must have knowledge of what all other wedding vendors are capable or not capable of and consider it when giving information to your clients. No matter how much a bride wants something, if it is impossible you must not promise it. It will only make you or the other vendors look bad and your bride will be unhappy.

On the other hand, if you are asked for something that is out of the ordinary, top planners and vendors will try to make it happen using creative solutions. Very little is truly impossible, especially if one has the resources to effectuate it, so stay open to trying new ways to do things.

Top wedding coordinators are prepared for wedding emergencies by carrying a myriad of things with them to solve such emergencies. You should assemble and carry an emergency kit that contains such diverse items as adhesive bandages, facial tissue, black socks for the men, bobby pins, safety pins, hairspray and on and on. Some coordinators find a suitcase with wheels the ideal way to carry their kit, while others have theirs in a nice looking shoulder bag. If you decide to carry any over the counter drugs such as aspirin or other pain relievers make sure you have them in unopened individual packages.

Assistants

There should be at least one assistant wedding coordinator at each wedding. Larger weddings or those in venues that are harder to manage should have the appropriate number of assistants to handle the needs of the particular wedding. Generally one assistant per one hundred guests is a good rule of thumb. However certain venues require more staff because of their physical layout. If, for example, the ceremony site is some distance from the reception site, several assistants must be stationed to direct the guests as they make their way between the locales if the venue does not provide such staff.

Assistants must dress and behave as professionally as the rest of the vendor team. New coordinators will often assist at a wedding of an established coordinator in order to learn the ropes. I have a written protocol for assistants stating what I expect of them in the way of behavior and attire. A copy of that is in Forms section in the back of this book under "Protocol for Assistants".

Rehearsals

An integral part of the wedding ceremony is the rehearsal. It is usually conducted in the ceremony location a day or two before the wedding. As the coordinator it is your job to conduct the rehearsal unless the wedding is in a church or temple and an in-house wedding director or the officiant directs it. Some officiants attend the rehearsal but most do not. A rehearsal should take no more than an hour. Any longer than that and you have a bored and restless group.

If the wedding ceremony is outside a place of worship, it is your job to contact the officiant well in advance to obtain all the information you need to properly direct the rehearsal, especially if the officiant will not be attending. Ascertain in advance if any props are necessary and which you, the venue or the couple are responsible for providing. Examples are the need for a table, a riser, a microphone, wine and/or glasses for a wine ceremony or candles and matches for a unity candle.

Anyone going down the aisle should attend the rehearsal. This includes people being formally seated or those walking in the procession. You and the bride and groom must determine in advance the order of the procession and where each participant will stand or be seated. The rehearsal is not the time to confer about this and wastes everyone's time while you have little private conferences or change things over and over again. It also confuses the participants when you make too many changes. It makes you appear unorganized - the kiss of death for a coordinator's reputation.

Start the rehearsal by addressing the entire group and introduce yourself. Explain what you are going to be doing on the wedding day and make any general announcements that all should be aware of. Speak in a loud and clear voice. Besides establishing you as an authority figure it gives all participants the opportunity to know what is expected of them. It should go without saying that you must dress professionally at the rehearsal. It is the first time many of the wedding party will meet you, and you want to consistently send the message of your professionalism.

Line the wedding party up in the front and explain the ceremony to them. You don't have to go through the whole thing word for word (this bores everyone and takes too much time) but just hit the highlights and practice any detailed parts such as lighting of candles. Then run through the entire processional from the protocol seating through the recessional so everyone learns the nuances. Offer to go through it again if the participants wish to, then let them go to their rehearsal dinner to celebrate.

I always gather the items needed on the wedding day from my brides at the rehearsal. I prepare a detailed list for them well in advance and take everything off their hands and minds at that time. This keeps confusion down on the wedding day and gives me a chance to go over all the items to make sure they are in usable form. For example, the place cards are alphabetized or the toasting glasses are washed with no stick on labels still affixed.

Ironclad Rule #20: **Make sure you know the whereabouts of the marriage license**.

You should have reminded the bride and groom of its importance months before the wedding. Giving them detailed information on how and where to obtain it in the area where the ceremony is taking place is an important part of your service for without it the ceremony will not be legal. (The actual signing and recording of the license complete the legal process.) I collect the license (along with the rest of the items on the list) and give it to the officiant if he/she has not already requested it from the bride and groom.

Disk Jockeys

A disk jockey (DJ), just as any master of ceremonies and music provider, can make or break a wedding reception. Top DJs are team players and know that they must take the lead from the wedding coordinator who is in charge of preparing the timeline for the event. When you get into the realm of high-end weddings most brides have a wedding coordinator they have been working with throughout the months of planning so it behooves you to learn to work with wedding coordinators if you are not already familiar with what they do.

Some disk jockeys pass themselves off as a wedding coordinator or tell bridal couples that they don't need a wedding coordinator as they will take care of making the timeline. This is not to say that you aren't capable of preparing a timeline for the flow of the reception, but a professional wedding coordinator does far more than that. Unless you are prepared to arrive at least two hours prior to the ceremony and perform such tasks as overseeing the room set up and the arrival of all vendors, pinning on boutonnieres, setting out the place cards and favors, greeting the arriving guests at the guest book table and bustling the bride's gown, not to mention assisting with all advance preparations such as ordering the invitations, cake and flowers and reserving the limousines, you are not a wedding coordinator in the true sense.

An illustrative way of looking at this is that wedding coordinators don't sell themselves as disk jockeys so disk jockeys shouldn't sell themselves as wedding coordinators. Everyone should do the job they specialize in. I certainly wouldn't want to be in charge of setting up equipment and playing music at a wedding I was directing.

As the MC you will work closely with the wedding coordinator and the banquet captain to make the reception flow smoothly. All three of you must be tuned in to everything that is happening at the reception at all times and must consult one another often to ensure a seamless event.

As a top DJ you must realize that a wedding reception is not a show that you are starring in but rather that you are there to make announcements and play appropriate music for each phase of the reception. The music during dinner should be chosen to allow conversation and all speakers are to be placed so that no one, especially a guest, is blasted out by them. Unless you are hired to do a stand-up comedy routine please do not do one or talk too much. Leave your ego at home. Please read the section under "Bands" entitled "Master of Ceremonies".

There is a distinct difference between a corporate party, a bar or bat mitzvah and a wedding reception and your dress and demeanor are different for each as well. Party props and silly dances and other guest participation activities can cheapen a wedding reception. Generally, higher-end or sophisticated brides are expressly opposed to having such things incorporated into their reception and during the planning phase when discussion of the type of DJ comes up, most brides and grooms specifically and emphatically say they want a sophisticated DJ and not one who's going to embarrass their guests or take over the party.

It's important to read the guests as the reception progresses and if that's not your strong point you must develop that sense. Because the music selection can set or change the mood you must be in tune with how the guests are responding to it. If you sense they are itching to dance you must play the type of music they want. If you sense they are enjoying the conversation you must be astute enough to let them do that. This is the kind of thing that separates a good DJ from a great one and being able to turn around on a dime can earn you a great reputation. Keep in mind that a wedding reception is a coming together of family and friends that will only happen in the same way this one time. Many people come from long distances to attend and conversation or visiting is often central to the event. It's up to you to make sure that the guests get what they came for while pleasing the bride and groom.

You must have well-kept, state of the art equipment the size of which is appropriate for the size of the room and crowd. Arrive in plenty of time to be completely set up for guests' entry into the room. Let the coordinator or the venue know in advance what you will need from them for your set-up, such as the size of table or number of dedicated circuits. Visit the venue in advance if necessary to become familiar with the loading dock or entry area , and don't try to enter through the front door with your equipment if there is a service entrance. Be especially mindful of where you leave your vehicle parked, both during load in and during the event. You must never block access for other vendors or assume that the parking space by the door is for you. It's probably empty for a good reason.

Ironclad Rule #15: (repeated) Appropriate music must be playing when the doors are formally opened for the guests.

The doors should not be opened unless the room is completely set up and this must be done timely. Observe safety precautions at all times and securely tape all cords and wires down to avoid any risk of injury to guests, the staff or yourself. Stow any equipment not a part of your set up out of sight and have your work area compact and neat.

Obtain all songs needed for the event in advance whether from your own collection, borrowed from the bride and groom (and returned at the end!) or purchased especially for the occasion. As the provider of music, it is your responsibility to coordinate this and you must notify the couple well in advance (this means days, not hours or minutes) if you cannot obtain something they have requested. Let's have no more horror stories of the DJ coming up to the bride and groom five minutes before their first dance and asking them to change it because you don't have the CD. That is utterly absurd.

If you are formally introducing the bride and groom and wedding party, be sure you know the correct pronunciation of their names. You should obtain in advance a list of their names with a phonetic pronunciation. Even apparently simple names can be pronounced differently than they look – for example is Bette pronounced "Betty" or "Bet"? Just before they enter you must come into the area outside the room and make sure they are lined up in the correct order and go over the pronunciation of their names again. It's a huge *faux pas* to mispronounce names, especially of the bride and groom.

At a small wedding of about 50 people the groom's eight year old son kept bugging the DJ to play a heavy metal song that he knew of which, by the way, was too advanced for the young fellow. The DJ resisted saying it was too early in the event to play such a song. He finally relented when the groom said he should play it to please the boy. However, it killed the party because it was too loud for the size of the room and the crowd and also because it was the wrong time to play it. The mistake was that the DJ considered this song the turning point in the music for the evening and kept it cranked up from then on. Some of the older guests literally fled the room because of the loudness and the party fell apart as the conversation ceased.

Remember that the people gathered here are their best friends who obviously know how to pronounce their names, so nearly everyone in the room will know you've made a mistake and over the microphone at that. By the way, it is not correct to introduce a couple as Mr. and Mrs. John and Jane Doe. It is either John and Jane Doe or Mr. and Mrs. John Doe. For some reason the former has crept into the vernacular but I'm hoping it will creep right out again.

As a Disk Jockey you have probably been listening to loud music for a long time because of your interest in it. As a result you might have some hearing loss, so I would suggest that you have your hearing checked periodically just to make sure that you can accurately hear the volume at which you are playing. In addition, you should invest in a decibel meter so you can be completely objective about the volume. One of the most common complaints I hear from guests at wedding receptions is that the music is too loud and I believe that some DJs aren't aware of how loud it is because they have lost part of their hearing. I actually carry ear plugs in my emergency kit to offer to guests who complain about the loud volume. But I would prefer the music to be at a level that would not precipitate their use.

Royalties are always a consideration when playing recorded music by professional artists. While it's beyond the scope of this book to go into the legalities of royalties, as a professional it is your responsibility to know the laws and honor them.

Read the section entitled "Bands" for further information.

Dove and butterfly providers

Doves and butterflies are used by some brides and grooms at the end of their wedding ceremony to add an element of beauty and surprise. It must be kept in mind that these are living creatures and must be treated with respect. The ultimate respect would be not to use any live creatures in this way, but if it is done care must be taken for their comfort. For example, they must be kept out of the sun and heat.

Doves

As a dove provider you will be present during the ceremony and most likely stationed near the front with your basket of birds to be released on a pre-arranged cue. You must dress inconspicuously to blend with the guests. Wear a neutral color (dark is best) as you will likely be in photographs taken during the ceremony.

In order to carry out the element of surprise to the guests as the doves are released you must arrive well before the ceremony and discreetly place the doves' cages or baskets at the point from where the release will be. Introduce yourself to the officiant or check in with the wedding planner to reconfirm the cue you will be given to open the cages. So as not to startle the bridesmaids and groomsmen or anyone else standing at the front of the ceremony it is important to let them know in advance that there will be a bird release. This information is usually imparted at the rehearsal by the planner.

Doves, which are actually homing pigeons, cannot be released too near sunset or they will not be able to orient themselves to find their home. They also should not be released in thunderstorms or very hot weather of over 100 degrees.

Butterflies

Butterflies are artificially raised for wedding releases then placed in small, individual boxes for distribution to guests who release them at a pre-determined signal during the ceremony. The butterflies are then supposed to simultaneously take flight making a beautiful, ethereal presence. However there are many instances where a guest has opened the box to find the butterfly dead, which puts a definite damper on that guest's enjoyment of the day and often all the festivities if there are more than a few dead butterflies.

Barbara Wallace

Some butterfly providers offer a guarantee that their insects will be alive but it is unlikely that most brides and grooms would know how many dead ones there were or even bother to try to enforce the guarantee. It also does not remove the negative feelings of a guest holding a dead or dying butterfly.

Once the boxed butterflies are shipped there is no way you as a provider can know what the purchaser does with them and even with explicit written instructions there is danger of mistreatment such as placement in a hot vehicle.

Favor providers

Some brides make their own favors but many order them from a source that provides either elements or the finished product all the way to delivery and even placement at the reception site. Favors are often edible items such as chocolates, and become a last minute task due to freshness. Whether edible or not, there are often intricate details in the wrapping of the favors.

Top favor providers are as professional as any other vendor and do not minimize the importance of that simply because their product is small in size. Sales, service and follow up are all important. Display and samples, including tastes of the product if it is edible, are essential.

Brides and grooms may have difficulty envisioning things, especially because they are seeing so much during the wedding planning process and are on overload. During the sales process you, as the favor provider, must listen carefully to your clients and try to suggest several ways to arrive at their vision. Making a prototype of the final one or two favor styles enables them to see an approximation of the finished product. If an edible product is being considered, it's a great sales tool to send home some samples to the groom or bride's parents who might not have attended the sales meeting. It's surprising how many times this clinches the decision.

If there is a décor designer, he or she should be consulted during the selection process as the kind of favor chosen will have impact on the overall design of the tabletops and contribute to the details of the wedding décor.

Delivery to the reception venue is an additional service and you can charge for it and for assistance with the placement of the favors at each place setting. Brides are often very happy to have this last minute service and will feel very comfortable if it is confirmed a day or so in advance.

The final product must be exactly as ordered and any monograms or names and dates must be checked for accuracy well in advance to avoid any rush do-overs or worse, too little time to fix the errors.

I suggest that heavily perfumed candles or other items be avoided if they are being set at each place setting as strong scents can interfere with the taste of food and some people have allergies to scents.

129

Florists

A top florist must have talent and creativity but that is just the beginning. When a client is spending anywhere from 10 to 30 percent of the entire wedding budget on flowers and decor they deserve both beautiful flowers AND professionalism.

Whether a very small operation with a garage based business or a large company with big name floral designers, professionalism is the element that separates the top florists from the also-rans. I have seen small companies with talented designers outperform large companies based purely on their outstanding service and understanding of the importance of professionalism.

From the first contact with a client to the last part of the strike it's important to be on time, professionally attired and unobtrusive. Here, chronologically, is a discussion of how you might conduct your business:

Planning stage

The initial client contact is a meeting that should take place in a comfortable, well lighted room with a table large enough to spread out books and photo portfolios of your prior work. As you inquire about the client's preferences <u>listen</u> to her and take notes as she describes her vision. Don't brag about yourself - at least not just yet.

Some florists have their work in albums separated by style or item (such as all tropicals or all bouquets or boutonnieres), others show full weddings to illustrate the breadth of their talent. You can do both and either way is fine as long as the client can see some of your finished products. It is important that you show your own work, not just pictures in popular books or magazines, though they can help, too. Often the bride has clipped some out herself. See the section on "Your Portfolio" for more information on the importance of photos.

The initial meeting usually lasts about one hour to an hour and a half. If you are finding you're spending more time than this, look at your sales pitch and streamline it. You don't want to give away too much information or design the whole wedding until the client has contracted you. However, you will want to show your creativity by suggesting ideas that generate some excitement and indicate that you are catching her vision.

Once you have finished the meeting and determined that the client wants a proposal from you, prepare that proposal as soon as possible, preferably within two or three days of the meeting. If you know at the meeting that you will not be able to turn the proposal out that quickly, tell the client and explain why. For example, there is a rare flower you must check availability of or the weekend coming up you are working on three weddings. If you have many details to confirm, such as availability of certain props that depend on sub-contractors, you should explain that this may cause you a delay. A client wants to hear back from you quickly. You must show them you care about their wedding and a quick response says that to them.

The proposal should clearly state, line by line, each item with a simple description of the style, colors and flowers and a price with a grand total including tax and delivery, set up and strike. Itemizing allows the client to cut or add things without being confused as to what will happen to her final price. You should explain that the price estimate is flexible and that she can control it by having less (or more!) flowers or fewer of the more expensive flowers. Some florists write a very flowery (pun intended) proposal, painting word pictures by description, but too much of this can overwhelm or confuse the client and can even delay the proposal's timely presentation. As a planner, I find that succinct descriptions are much easier to comprehend when reviewing a proposal, and I want the result to jump out at me rather than having to wade through wordy descriptions. Many clients are not familiar with the names of flowers or other terminology in the florist's world so get even more bogged down.

The proposal should be neatly typed on a word processor for ease in revisions and sent or presented in a nice envelope unless it is e-mailed as an e-mail attachment (not in the body of the e-mail itself as it will never arrive lined up in a uniform manner), which is something many brides prefer today. Presentation is an important yet subtle step in establishing your professionalism to the bride. The best florists also automatically send a copy of the proposal to the wedding planner - an impressive habit.

One florist presented such a detailed and convoluted proposal that I actually had a client throw it away in frustration because she couldn't make sense of it. On the other hand, I often refer one florist who pulls out a calculator at the end of the initial meeting and gives a reasonably accurate estimate before she leaves.

You don't want to provide so many details in the proposal that a client can take your proposal and shop it to other, less ethical florists, who will promise to beat your prices while copying your designs. (See the section on "Ethics" if you think copying the work or ideas of others is an acceptable way to do business.)

Many, probably most, brides (and some wedding planners, tsk, tsk) do not call a vendor if they decide not to hire them. They do not seem to realize that it is rude, so following up with the client or her wedding planner after a couple of weeks has gone by is a good business practice. It is a good idea to have an expiration date on your proposal or to state that the date is not confirmed until a deposit is received. In other words, don't promise to hold the date and then turn away another potential client with the possible outcome that the first one doesn't book you after all.

Once the client has agreed to hire you, get a substantial down payment of from 30 to 50%. See the section on "Deposits" above for a discussion on buying the date from you and the client's commitment. It's always a good idea to include a clause in the contract that you will take all reasonable steps to supply the plant material that the bride desires but that certain conditions, such a grower's inability or shipping issues might prevent it and reasonable substitutions will be made. Obviously, anytime your product depends upon another's product you must protect yourself.

One florist who forgot to verify the final count of the wedding party just before the wedding came up one bouquet short. This was not discovered until he began handing out the bouquets to the bridesmaids just before photos. He had already sent the excess flowers back to his shop so that bridesmaid ended up carrying a quickly assembled tray of items that related to the wedding. Of course, the guests thought it was planned that way- but what bride or vendor needs that kind of stress at the last minute? A simple verification would have avoided that drama.

A final planning meeting is held about two weeks prior to the wedding date at which time most florists ask for the final payment and make sure they understand the bride's vision exactly. It is also the time when final table and wedding party counts are given, though it is important to remain flexible if there are last minute changes even a day or two before the wedding. You can also verify more accurately which floral material will be available on the wedding day and discuss possible substitutions that might be necessary.

Wedding day

Timely arrival is one of the primary requirements on the wedding day. If you have not worked at the wedding and/or reception venue before, ascertain in advance just exactly how to access the loading dock and allow plenty of time for your load-in. On a busy weekend in a major hotel the loading dock can be a nightmare that deducts precious minutes from your set up time. Or you might have to carry your arrangements up stairs or through long hallways or use miniscule elevators that can eat up your precious installation time.

Know in advance where the personal flowers are to be delivered and take them there per the pre-arranged schedule. The photographer most likely will want them distributed and pinned on in time to start the family and group photos and it is up to you to know the time and place. If the planner does not call you, you must call her to find out. Make sure that personal flowers are grouped by where they are going rather than by gender. For example, the bride's dad and other male members of her family will most likely be with her than with the groom and groomsmen so you should probably send their boutonnieres with the bride's flowers instead of with the other men's flowers.

Ironclad Rule #21: <u>Always</u> clearly label <u>every</u> personal floral item by either the job or the person's name (or both) by some means that will not fall off.

This is extremely important and too often overlooked. Determine in advance just who will be responsible for pinning on the boutonnieres and corsages (they might expect it to be you or your staff). The photographer or the wedding planner or an assistant might pin on the flowers and they have little or no idea who the recipients are, especially in a large wedding party or extended family where many are being honored with flowers. Several labeling ideas top wedding florists have used are having each item in its own clear plastic bag or box with the label affixed, or pinning a small label with the name on it to each stem with a straight pin. Having loose labels placed next to each flower is not acceptable as once the flower is picked up and not pinned on it is likely to be put back down in an entirely different place making that labeling system no better that no label at all. I can't tell you how many times there have been no labels at all on the personal flowers. Remember, a wedding planner or photographer cannot divine this information and it's unfair to have them delayed because you didn't label the flowers properly.

Make sure there is at least one pin with each corsage and boutonniere – the larger heavier corsage may require two pins. The pins for the boutonnieres should have black tips and be shorter than the pearl headed corsage pins so they do not show under the jacket lapels. Always pin starting under the lapel and come through the flower stem then back down and into the back of the lapel. I have seen flowers pinned on with the head of the pin showing and this looks especially bad with the white pearl headed pin on a black tuxedo. If you are the designated pinner, practice in advance so you can do it quickly and efficiently when a group is watching you and they are being summoned by the photographer.

> One top florist I frequently refer makes an extra complimentary boutonniere for the groom so his can be replaced half way through the day when the original one is smashed from the many hugs he has received.

Set up should be as neat and quick as possible. Do as much as possible in advance at your shop. It is not professional to build all your arrangements on site unless you have arranged in advance for your own behind-the-scenes staging area that will act as an auxiliary shop for the event. Top wedding florists work very neatly and keep the public areas organized and free of extraneous items. Strewing your tools and trash over the site gives onlookers and passersby the impression that you are amateurish and not in control and also makes for more cleanup work at the last minute. Always bring a tarpaulin or clean white sheet on which to work and place it as far from the public view as is convenient for your set up. This enables you to simply wrap it up and carry it away without a major problem, especially if time becomes short.

Common sense dictates that you begin your set up with the areas that will be seen first by arriving guests then work inward. Obviously the ceremony will be prior to the reception so complete that area first then move into the reception area taking your tools and mess with you.

Be sure to have a broom and/or rake as part of your tool kit so you can clean up efficiently. Bring your own ladder if you even remotely think you will need one. Don't rely on the house to supply one which could cause you a delay. Due to safety and liability issues many venues won't let you use their ladder even if they have it close by. With your own ladder you'll know it is safe. The rest of your tool kit should be planned to make you as self-sufficient as imaginable.

Ironclad Rule #22: **Never have to rely on someone else to carry out your duties efficiently.**

Always check with the wedding coordinator or other person in charge (e.g. bride, bride's mom, venue coordinator) before departing to make sure everything is done correctly and that nothing is missing. Better to correct any problems now than to be summoned back when you're miles away and time is short. Many florists make and leave an extra boutonniere or two that can even be used as a corsage in a pinch. A small flower is better than none at all when it comes to honoring someone special on the wedding day. You might also leave a few loose flowers and petals in case of an emergency. More than once I've had to patch up something using those extra flowers.

After the wedding

Top wedding florists <u>always</u> plan to move any flowers or décor after the ceremony to the reception as part of their job. Do not expect the groomsmen, the wedding planner or the housemen to do it (or worse yet ignore that it needs to be considered). Include the price of it in your proposal starting with the first draft.

If you are to be seen by any guests during this flower relocation process, you must wear proper attire so that you blend in with the guests at least to some degree. If there is more than one worker, a uniform looks best and it can be as simple as khaki pants and a white polo shirt with an apron over it or all black. Please don't wear jeans and hanging out tee-shirts and look like you just walked in from a day of working in your yard.

Plan the route in advance so you avoid or at least minimize being seen by guests. This is backstage stuff and the guests should not see what's going into making their experience a beautiful one.

If you have to come back to pick up props and rental items after the ceremony or reception be sure to determine in advance just when it will be finished. Top florists do not enter if the party is still going on (exception- if the band has finished playing and some guests are lingering and just don't want to go home) nor do they wait too long and risk losing their props or inconveniencing the venue whose housemen might be trying to turn the room for an immediately following function. Most venues do not have storage facilities and it is your responsibility to collect and inventory your things in a timely manner. Discuss who pays for missing and broken props in advance with your client so there is no misunderstanding about this in the end. Props left for protracted periods of time are very likely going to disappear either because of being stolen, mistaken for trash because of being abandoned or innocently stored by the facility who mistakenly believes it to be theirs.

Additional services

Some florists offer linen and chair cover rental and lighting services as part of their décor options which are often desired by high-end clients. If you choose to do that you can either sub-contract them for installation by that vendor, rent them and have your crew install them, own the stock which you warehouse yourself, or a combination of these. Whichever method you choose must be carried out as professionally as the rest of your business. You may decide to take a markup on sub-contracted items that pays you for handling them which is an acceptable and common practice. However, some wedding planners also offer these items so be careful you are not infringing on the territory of the person who referred you to the client.

Clients love to see the linens, centerpiece, chairs and other components on a table with a portion of the room decoratively lighted. It's expensive to do this prior to being contracted so I don't necessarily recommend that, but when it comes down to making final choices, especially for the higher end weddings, scheduling a demonstration of the room set up is very effective and can even result in additional sales when the client sees how great it all looks.

Gowns

The white wedding gown exemplifies a bride as no other thing does and there is such magic in a bridal gown. It is probably the most expensive article of clothing a woman will ever purchase and will most likely be worn only once which is actually quite amazing.

Manufactured/Ready-To-Wear

Often the first thought of a newly engaged bride is to shop for her gown. It seems that everyone is aware of the long lead time involved before delivery of the finished product and horror stories abound. Thus it is extremely important for the bridal gown salon to quell any fears, whether real or imagined. However, it is also important to be honest about the delivery lead time and frankly discuss rush charges if they might apply.

Outstanding service is the most important thing for you as a top bridal salon to offer your clients as there are usually several stores that carry the same styles. You must have experienced sales women on staff who behave professionally with the bride's best interest in mind at all times. A bride should never get the impression that your store wants the sale just for the sake of the profit involved and if, indeed, you do not have the right thing – whether in style or price range - for the bride, you should politely refer her to a store to which she is better suited.

Because the bridal gown is so important to most brides they might go to half a dozen stores to try on gowns and may come back several times. You must realize that this is common and in the end, all other things being equal, the bride will chose from the place where she feels most comfortable. Playing games such as pretending not to know who the designer is or lying about the store's exclusivity are

> I once heard a seamstress bragging about how she had posed as the bride's aunt and spent time in the dressing room of an exclusive bridal salon examining an expensive gown from the inside so she could approximate the construction. I was appalled that, first of all, her lack of ethics would allow her to do such a thing and, second, that she would then brag openly about it. I suspect the salon knew exactly what this group was up to. In fact, they probably knew from the moment they walked in the door that they were not legitimate customers. That seamstress is the kind of wedding vendor that I keep on my private "do not refer" list.

unprofessional behaviors and will give your store a bad name - later if not sooner.

Most gown stores, whether free-standing or a department in a large department store, have a niche and market to the bride they buy for. It's impossible to be all things to all brides so finding and marketing your niche well is as important in gowns as it is in any other service. By focusing on that niche, the brides you want will eventually come to you.

Most stores will not allow a bride to be photographed in a gown before it is purchased. This is to protect themselves from the ethically challenged bride who might be trying to copy an expensive gown by having it made by an outside seamstress.

Once the gown has been selected, following up with the client is very important so the bride knows exactly when to expect her gown for the first fitting, and any delays should be discussed as soon as the salon knows about them and before the bride has to call and inquire about the status of her gown. You must keep in mind that, to the bride, she is the most important customer the salon has and this is her big purchase for her big day. If your salon can treat all their customers as if that were true you will earn a wonderful reputation and practically be guaranteed success.

Sample gowns can get shop worn very quickly when they are tried on over and over again by brides of all sizes but it is important to keep the gowns in as good a condition as possible. Being presented with a dirty gown to try on leaves a poor impression on a bride subconsciously, even if she consciously knows the gown is in such condition because it has been "well loved". Doing some periodic spot cleaning and simple mending will do wonders in keeping the gowns looking presentable and might give your store the edge it needs to close a sale.

Sample gowns are usually in size 10, which actually means nothing, because one designer's size 10 is different than another's and it is rumored that this is closer to a regular size 8. Actually, the gowns are ordered by the bride's body measurements and almost all must have some alterations.

Top gown salons have expert seamstresses in their alterations department who interact professionally with brides as well as do a great sewing job. Much of the seamstresses' job is performed in the back room but she must be presentable when it is time to come out for fittings. If she is sloppy or dour the image of the store will suffer. She must never say anything negative about a bride's shape or body type in front of the bride or anyone connected with her family or wedding party.

Alterations charges are often substantial particularly if there is beading or intricate decoration that must be replaced. Some stores charge a flat rate of about $450 to $500 that covers all alterations and anything greater than that is absorbed by the store. Other stores have a reputation for ordering gowns in the incorrect size so they can make more profit in alterations. It doesn't take much to figure out which store is better regarded in the community.

One horror story I witnessed was a seamstress who told a bride at her second fitting that she was getting fat and there wouldn't be anymore material left to let the gown out if she kept gaining weight. The bride was reduced to tears on the fitting platform – not a very nice memory of the gown that's supposed to be worn on the happiest day of one's life. Another bride was told by the fitter that the gown was fine- it was her body that was misshapen resulting in tears for that bride, too. The upshot of the latter story is that the gown was taken to a talented tailor who made the bride – who by the way had a lovely figure – feel, and look, like a princess in her wedding gown.

Custom/Couture

Most brides look to a custom gown only after they have tried on several ready-to-wear bridal gowns and have no luck in finding "the" gown. By then, they probably have as much an idea of what they don't want as what they do want.

Some brides don't have the self-confidence to have a wedding gown custom made. The bride might not have enough experience in choosing fabrics or may not know her body well enough to select the best style for herself thinking "what if I don't like it when it's done?" However, for those with the self-confidence, a custom gown can be a wonderful way to get a one of a kind gown with a perfect fit.

The custom designer must be a great fitter and seamstress as well as a talented designer. Having a well photographed portfolio of gowns that he or she has completed is imperative, as is having an ample supply of fabric swatches and the ability to obtain more in a reasonable length of time. Swatches large enough to be draped on the client's body are optimal but at the least should be large enough to display the texture and qualities of the fabric.

Expect to be asked for references by prospective brides. If possible, arrange in advance with former clients to allow inquiries. Many brides love to talk about their wedding after it's over and will gush over you if you did an outstanding job for them.

Having a clean, uncluttered studio/showroom is consistent with being a top custom gown designer. Décor should be simple and in keeping with the image you wish to portray. Several comfortable chairs and a table on which to spread out pictures and swatches are important. Most brides are accompanied by their mom or a good friend - sometimes more than one - and their comfort will add to the overall experience. Several mirrors, at least one three way, are imperative, as is good light, preferably natural. Have gown samples to try on and provide a large, private dressing area with enough hooks to hold the bride's street clothes and all the gowns she's trying on and a three way mirror. If your actual workroom is on the premises, keep the sewing area/workroom with its myriad scraps and lint behind closed doors. It keeps the showroom neater and also adds a bit of mystique that can conjure up mental images of exclusivity.

You, as the designer, must work to get the vision of the dream gown. Listening to the bride is the first step. Encourage her to bring photos of gowns or elements of gowns that she likes. Even crude sketches can help you visualize her vision. Sketches and fabric swatches are then shown. As with any design process, it's important not to "give away the store" in the planning process before the contract is drawn but care must be taken to convey the designer's competence and creativity in order to build the client's trust. If you are adept at rendering you can do one or two of the final choices, but that would probably be after the contract is signed.

One top custom wedding gown designer I know makes all fitting appointments as soon as the contract is signed. Her goal is to finish the gown about one month before the wedding and she works backward from there and sets mutually convenient appointments with her clients. Besides being efficient it shows the bride clearly what her time commitment will be and allows her to schedule her other appointments around her fittings rather than trying to squeeze them in when her time is tighter as the wedding draws nearer.

Alterations/Bridesmaids Dresses

Alterations are necessary in almost all wedding gowns ranging from a simple hem shortening to very complex fitting and re-beading. Most bridal salons offer alterations to their customers but some brides choose not to use them for one reason or another. If you offer bridal alterations you must conduct your business as professionally as any other wedding vendor in order to become a top alterationist.

Bridesmaid or flower girl dresses are more commonly custom sewn than the wedding gown itself. Some brides do not want such dresses to be custom designed but merely sewn to order so need a seamstress rather than a couturier. They are still looking for as professional an operation as described above. Depending on the needs of your clientele you might construct the garments from patterns and fabric they bring you or you might offer complete service, including obtaining fabrics.

If you sew for wedding party attendants you will find that often at least some of the participants are from out of town so might be long distance or last minute clients or both. Allow for this and make sure you can deliver as promised before taking the job. Sometimes you will have to begin the job from measurements provided by the client and have a fitting later in the process so be sure you are capable of doing that, and allow enough time for last minute changes if the participant is coming in only a day or so before the wedding. It is important that you not contribute any stress to the wedding plans by delaying delivery of the job as promised. That would ruin your reputation faster than you can imagine.

Pressing

For a bride whose wedding is in the town where she resides, gown pressing is not much of an issue because the gown will be pressed just before she picks it up from the store or designer shortly before her wedding. However, for a destination bride whose gown must be carried onto a plane, last minute pressing can be an issue. Professional gown pressing is an important service, especially in an area with many destination weddings. The gown often has to be transported on an airplane and no matter how well pressed before packing and how well packed, it's bound to have a least a few wrinkles.

Most brides rightly fear entrusting their gown to the hotel's cleaning department so as a top gown presser and a top notch seamstresses you can offer a pressing service in which you come to the hotel with your iron and/or steamer and press all gowns the day before the wedding. The better hotels can provide a rack of some kind on which to hang the gowns to dry after the steaming. As the "on location" presser, you must be prompt and professional in both demeanor and attire.

You must be so well versed in fabrics and fibers that you know the properties of each and whether steam can be used or just a dry iron. You must also be sure enough of your knowledge and ability that you can confidently tackle the pressing of a gown that costs $10,000 or more. It's important to have a contract for this kind of work as it is for any other and liability insurance is imperative based upon the fact that you are handling expensive gowns and fine fabrics. Ruining a wedding gown the day before the wedding would ruin the wedding so you must be well covered for your own protection.

Never leave the pressing job until you have gone over the finished product with the bride just to make sure she's pleased with the result. I once had a presser who had to return to the hotel after she was a half hour away because the bride thought her gown's train needed additional pressing when it was on the hanger. It was actually fine when it was on her body but it took a return trip for the presser to show her that in person.

A good marketing method if you are interested in building a pressing clientele is to introduce yourself to the hotel's catering departments to make them aware of your service. Top notch hotels are always looking for the best vendors for their guests' needs even if this means going outside the hotel for the service.

Preservation

Many brides are not aware of the importance of preserving the wedding gown immediately following the wedding. While it is unlikely that the gown will ever be worn again it's important to clean it, even if it will just be stored and brought out every few years to look at. Removal of unseen stains such as sugar, white wine and perspiration will prevent much of the yellowing that occurs when these stains oxidize over months and years of storage.

As a top gown preservationist you must first be an expert cleaner but you must also treat each wedding gown uniquely and handle it separately from other items that are being cleaned. Naturally it does not go into a vat of cleaning solution along with other items that might be being cleaned that day. Any minor rips or tears are mended and major damage is discussed with the bride especially if the result will not look exactly like the original product. Any stains, such as red wine, that might not be successfully be removed should also be discussed with the client.

The charge for the cleaning and preservation must be discussed in advance with your bride. You'll probably have a minimum charge for the simplest gowns which increases depending on the complexity of the design and fabric. Some cleaners quote the final fee only after they have received the gown and assessed the work involved. They don't start the cleaning until the bride approves it, offering to send the gown back at their expense if she does not.

The cleaned gown is packed in an acid-free box surrounded with acid-free tissue that can be opened for viewing and refolding. In fact, a "hermetically sealed" or "airtight" box is actually bad for the gown in the long run because the fabric cannot breathe and such packaging must be avoided. You might consider including a pair of new white cotton gloves that can be used to handle the gown when viewing is desired just as is done with museum quality preserved apparel.

Most top gown preservationists provide the proper shipping box, which is postage paid and insured, to the client so the gown can easily be sent for preservation and cleaning. They also include the return postage and insurance in the quoted fee so when the cleaned gown is sent back the deal is complete.

Following up with the bride is important. All brides want to know when they can expect their gown back so give a time estimate at the outset. If you are more generous with the estimate and the gown is finished early the bride will be delighted. If there is a delay, keep the bride apprised so she knows you are on top of it. Always make sure you have the proper address for returning the gown since many newlyweds relocate. That is something to check at the outset and double check just before sending.

Hair dressers and makeup artists

A woman who might not ordinarily wear much makeup or put her hair in an updo will often have both done for her wedding day. However, she might be nervous about it for fear of looking overly done up or unlike herself.

The best bridal hair and makeup artists provide an unhurried preview for the bride, often months before the wedding, during which they take extensive notes. You might draw the colors and styles onto a diagram of a face so that on the wedding day you can copy exactly what the bride decided upon during the preview. You might even take a digital or Polaroid photo of the finished product for the bride's file.

The preview is generally not a free service unless you, as the artist, are a representative of a makeup line at a store counter. Many top artists only do a preview after the client is booked and include that in the price quotation. For this reason it is important that you have an extensive portfolio of your work so the bride feels comfortable with your style and ability. References from former brides are also helpful and some brides like to talk to your former clients.

Previews can be held in a salon or even the home of the client if both you and the client are comfortable there and mirrors and lighting are adequate. Some artists exclusively do bridal hair and makeup on location and hold previews at their place of business which is set up just for that purpose. If you are a hairdresser who works in a full service salon, being out of your salon can take you away from your regular clientele for a good part of the day (usually a Saturday) which becomes considerable lost revenue on a typically busy day. This must be factored into your fee structure and you might impose minimums on the services you will go on location for.

Ironclad Rule #23: **It is absolutely and unequivocally imperative that you be on time on the wedding day.**

Being on time is the most important factor in the hair and makeup artist's arsenal. No excuses are acceptable. No matter how talented you are, or how beautiful you can make a bride look, if she is late for the photographs or other wedding day activities you can throw the entire day off and will stress out the entire wedding party, not to mention getting on the bad side of the planner and photographer.

Because the atmosphere in the room can be volatile and full of emotions and family dynamics, you must be a paragon of calmness and control. You have the ability to diffuse situations that could spin out of control and can work with the coordinator or other responsible person to redirect them. If you are hyper or histrionic or like to intensify a tense situation you're in the wrong business. It would do us all a favor if you stay in the salon where your behavior isn't quite so disruptive.

Referrals are an important part of the makeup artist and hairdresser's business so your reputation for professional behavior and timeliness are as important as talent.

Cleanliness is very important and the top makeup and hair providers are meticulous about it. Makeup artists and hair dressers must be state licensed and insured just as any other top wedding vendor is. The application of a substance to someone's face and scalp contains inherent liability issues and the proper training and awareness is the first step in avoiding any issues with that. Make sure the client is aware of the manner in which you carry out the maintenance of your equipment and the thorough cleaning and/ or disinfecting of any permanent applicators before the next use.

It is important to remember that professional attire is imperative here. What is hip in a salon often looks too casual for "on location" wedding day work. Please refer to the section in Part II entitled "Appearance/Dress".

Whether or not you sell makeup or skin care products is a business decisions. I personally do not like to refer a hairdresser or makeup artist that does because I don't want my brides to feel pressured into buying them, and the perception is that you are not objectively providing them with the best product for their needs.

Ice Sculptors

An ice sculpture can add a lovely focal point to a wedding reception and can be as simple as a centerpiece for an hors d'oeuvre display to an elaborate multi-level creation.

I once had a florist bring flowers in an ice vase which was set into a shallow tray, the capacity of which could never have held the melted ice. Much focus was on the resulting water during the entire event and several servers and I spent time sopping it up to avoid a mini flood. The vase quickly developed a hole in one side and ultimately became unusable which meant that there was no container for the flowers which landed in a sink for lack of a better place to put them.

Most ice sculptures are provided through the reception venue as part of the food service order and might be obtained through an outside contractor who specializes in ice carving. Other times a wedding planner will order the sculpture and in a few instances a bride will go direct to the sculptor. Clearly, most often the client will be another wedding professional and with that comes the prospect of repeat business.

No matter where the business comes from, you as the ice sculptor must be as professional as any other wedding vendor, which means returning phone calls, following up with clients, being insured, being properly attired and adhering to all other things that set the top wedding vendors apart from average as described in the beginning of this book. Obviously your artistic talent is important, but without the professionalism to sustain you the talent could be overshadowed.

Technical skills are highly important in designing and setting up ice displays and outside of the beauty of the sculpture the most important consideration is "where is all that water going to go when it melts?" Common sense dictates that there must be provisions made for a container of a larger capacity than the volume of water from the melted ice otherwise the floor will be flooded. The result of course could be dangerous as well as unattractive and just plain messy.

If using ice displays to actually hold dishes or food, the shelf-life of the ice container must be considered, as melting ice will get very slippery and even a flat surface can change shape. Trays can tumble as the shape of the ice changes. Adding glass to that mix could result in breakage which would then render all the food in the immediate vicinity unusable as the assumption must be made that invisible glass shards contaminated it.

A top ice sculptor is an artist who can provide prospective clients with sketches or renderings to illustrate the ideas they are discussing. Some clients (whether the planner or the bride and groom) will have a basic idea of the look they want to achieve and you can assist with the design process by pointing out both the pros and cons of the concepts as they come together at the optimal end product. You should not be afraid to give your input as you are the expert in the field and can bring much to the table – in fact you are expected to do so.

Delivery and set up must be coordinated with the venue in advance so you are sure of the logistical issues. You must make arrangements for any props that are part of the sculpture or set up to be retrieved by your crew in a timely manner at the end of the event or risk losing them. If you expect maintenance issues during the event, either discuss them in advance with the catering manager or banquet captain or have your own properly attired staff there to handle them.

Invitation Providers

Wedding invitations can vary from the traditional white engraved card to a quite elaborate multi-part custom set that reflects the uniqueness of the wedding couple. Whatever the style chosen, wedding invitations are one element of the wedding that seems to be surrounded with etiquette-related mysteries. As a top invitation provider you are expected to be very well versed in wedding invitation etiquette and to know most of the correct answers off the top of your head. For the more arcane answers you must be armed with an arsenal of reference books which you can consult on the spot.

Time is of the essence in the wedding invitation business, especially for the wedding with a short planning phase. It is imperative that a written timetable be established right away by working backwards from the wedding day and considering time for refining the guest list, designing, ordering, printing, addressing, which might include calligraphy, and assembling. You might manage all phases while keeping your client informed as to the client's next responsibility in the process. Make sure the client has a copy of the timetable so they clearly see what deadlines they must uphold to keep the process moving.

Your place of business should be comfortable and uncluttered with a table large enough to spread out several of the large catalogs that usually accompany the sale of invitations. You must be very familiar with the lines you carry so you can guide the bride in zeroing in on both her wants and needs. That way you can show her the proper style without having her be overwhelmed with the myriad choices. Listening to her vision for her wedding is an important first step.

Because the wedding invitation sets the pace for the rest of the wedding and is a way for the guests to get an idea the formality of the event, it is important that the selection of the invitation be carefully thought out and appropriate. Working with the bride's wedding coordinator can be a big help and full service planners might attend the invitation sessions as part of the wedding design process. When a unique invitation is desired, the whole design look must be considered and the planner's input is of the utmost importance. Consider even the choice of stamps as they will add to the overall look of the invitation.

Checking and re-checking the order forms you will send to the printer is imperative. Having the client review and initial the final order form is also imperative. Both of you must look for misspellings and format errors and, if there is time, a proof of the final printing is a good idea especially in the more costly sets. Having to do an order over is not only time consuming but can eat up all your profit if you are at fault. Naturally mistakes will occur from time to time – it's a fact of being human. But too many mistakes can harm your reputation. However, how you handle mistakes can actually enhance your reputation if you go the extra mile to correct them.

If you are managing the addressing for your client make sure they know at the outset how to format their guest list so the calligrapher can use it most efficiently. An Excel spreadsheet is an efficient way that can also be utilized by the client to track their wedding gifts and thank you notes and more.

Customer service is very important in the invitation business. Many retailers carry the same invitation books because, after all, there are only so many commercial printers out there. Thus, outstanding customer service and your superior knowledge can become the defining factor in making your business successful.

Some invitation sellers offer discounts of from 10 to 25% off the catalog price. However, discounting things is not consistent with being a high end vendor and if you go out of your way to provide exemplary service you should be compensated for it by getting your full profit margin. The final decision on discounting is up to you, of course.

A colleague wedding coordinator told me of an experience she had with an invitation provider who made a mistake on the wedding program. She reprinted them and they were barely ready in time to be taken to the church to be passed out at the ceremony. Even though it was her mistake, she expected the coordinator to pick them up and wouldn't go out of her way to deliver them. Guess who that coordinator never referred again?

Custom invitations are often desired by high end clients as they want, and are willing to pay for, something that no one has ever seen before. If you offer that service all of the above parameters apply with the addition of more design meetings with both the client and the planner and even the décor designer. You must have an arsenal of unusual papers and resources for less common printing methods, such as letterpress, along with your unique ideas. Your clients will expect prototypes and mock ups presented to them in a professional and timely manner.

Your office and staff must be organized so changes (and there will be many, often minute changes) are noted and incorporated. Having one person assigned to a client is far more efficient than having too many people involved and risking having things fall through the cracks. The details are where you can shine, but not catching them can also be your downfall, so it is imperative that you stay on top of this at all times.

There might be intricate assembly so it is important that you have a crew that understands that you expect perfection from the finished product.

> You must also make sure that your more intricate designs actually work. One invitation designer came up with an innovative custom design but the guests' feedback was that they had a very difficult time determining how to open the card. A simple change in the design could have alleviated that had a prototype been thoroughly tested prior to manufacture.

Lighting Providers

More and more brides are realizing how important decorative lighting is to the overall design of the wedding, especially the reception, and are considering it when making their budget.

In some instances lighting will be part of the décor budget and will be managed by the décor designer. Other times the planner will arrange for and manage it. On rare occasions, the bride and groom will manage it themselves.

As a top lighting provider you must conduct your business professionally, just as any other outstanding wedding vendor does, with respect to returning phone calls promptly, sending proposals and contracts promptly, being appropriately attired and all other behavior as described in the beginning of this book.

Because lighting is something fewer people are aware of, having an excellent portfolio is important so brides and grooms can see the impact of your lighting in a room. The best lighting people are artists as well as technicians. Anyone with even a modicum of knowledge of electricity and lighting equipment can install lighting, but knowing the impact of colors, and the nuances they can create, is where artistry enters the picture and separates an adequate lighter from a great one. There must be something to the artistry issue or there wouldn't be an Academy Award for lighting.

I always wish for a photo where a room is shown with the ambient light on one side and the enhanced lighting on the other to illustrate just how great the centerpieces and cake look with a pinspot on them, or how much more atmosphere is attained with some beautifully placed uplights, for example.

For larger jobs, offering a lighting demonstration for the clients is a wonderful way to show how the reception room will look on their wedding day. Because many brides and grooms are not astute at visualizing décor, a demo is invaluable. A few months before the wedding, the planner can arrange for a table or two to be set with the linens and flowers and other décor items in a corner of the reception room which your lighting will enhance. The client has the opportunity to choose what they like best in all décor elements and it becomes an exciting experience for them. It's also a time for all the décor people to refine their final products to give the client the desired result.

It's important to differentiate a wedding from a corporate event when designing the lighting. Corporate events are often sales meetings or parties to hype the company so vibrant colors and unusual effects are desired while weddings usually require softer, more subtle effects. Here's where the artistry comes in.

When lighting a social event you must hide the mechanics as much as possible and cover any poles (light trees) with an appropriate color to blend them into the walls. In larger or newer venues you'll likely have ceiling hanging points that will keep poles to a minimum. You can offer an optional standby lighting technician on smaller jobs, but should require and include one when you price larger jobs. I also believe a dimmer is an important required addition rather than being optional. You must also be sure to include the necessity of a power drop in your initial proposal even if the client isn't paying you directly for it. They must be made aware that the venue could charge them for it. Surprises having to do with additional charges are generally not well received after the fact.

Safety must always be first in the lighting business. Lighting has so many dangerous components, beginning with the electricity itself and including cords, hanging lamps scaffolding, poles and heat, not to mention ladders and scissor lifts used for installation. Obviously, having copious insurance coverage is important for your company and your employees.

In planning décor installation, lighting is one of the first components to go in. Ideally the room would be empty but that is usually a luxury and lighting is installed while having to move the ladder between tables and chairs. Team work and a sense of humor are of the utmost importance in such a situation as the flower, linen and tree installers are all vying for the same space often in a short time frame, not to mention the housemen and the band roadies. Sometimes a venue will allow the lighting to be placed early so consider requesting that to alleviate the crush. Your crew must work neatly and replace exactly anything they had to move during installation.

As a top lighting company you must test every seat at every table to make sure that no guests will have a light shining in their eyes from the centerpiece pinspot or any other light source. You must also bring a full set of colored gels so you can change any and all the colors if necessary.

Some larger lighting companies don't want to be bothered lighting weddings but there can be a good bit of business from it, especially if you develop relationships with wedding planners and florists who become your repeat clients. There is nothing wrong with setting a minimum price for your lighting services. Once you have worked in a venue it's easier for you to do it the next time, and having photos of various venues will enable prospective clients to see their options. With enough photos you won't have to do a demo for every small client but might find that your service sells itself.

Limousine and Other Transportation Providers

Punctuality and honesty are very important traits of a limousine company and rate equally with well maintained vehicles. One thing a couple doesn't need on their wedding day is transportation that isn't dependable.

Top limousine companies always deliver what they promise and they only promise what they are sure they can deliver.

I have experienced such practices as a limo company telling a bride she's going to get a stretch Hummer then sending another stretch SUV saying the Hummer broke down, when in fact a bigger paying client wanted the Hummer. Or they might substitute a smaller or older or wrong color car because they fouled up when they did their scheduling. These are old tired excuses which are very transparent and can ruin a company's reputation fast.

As a top limousine company you must have professionally attired drivers with polished manners who know the route they are driving or obtain complete directions in advance. In this day and age of internet map programs and detailed paper maps there is absolutely no excuse for a limo driver not to know where he is going or to be late because he is lost. As part of the information obtained from the client or wedding coordinator, you must get complete driving instructions including directions to any difficult to find buildings or tricky traffic patterns. You must also get telephone numbers of key individuals, which might include the wedding coordinator's cell phone number as well as office number, the telephone number of the home or building where clients are to be picked up, and mobile phone numbers of other key players. You must either give those key people your driver's mobile number or a number for your dispatch which is operating the entire duration of the job so the driver can always be reached and tracked.

The paperwork you provide to your driver must clearly state his itinerary including all stops and backtracks or shuttling that is expected during the run. Such paperwork must also be given in advance to the wedding coordinator or other key people so everyone is aware of the timing and scheduling and whether the vehicle(s) are to stand or make a split run if there is a large time gap. Because there are often 3 to 5 hour minimums for bookings, especially on weekend nights, your limousine must be available to the client for the full time if they are being charged the minimum.

Arranging for payment in advance of the service is another hallmark of the top limousine providers. Do not expect the client to pay your driver on the day of service and to whip out a credit card before you proceed on the journey. That should all be taken care of in advance and be on file in the office. Clear paperwork is important with any overtime charges spelled out and taken care of after the fact by means of the credit card for which authorization has been obtained in advance. For the rare client that only pays with cash or for a last minute booking that must be paid on the spot, your driver should be as discreet as possible, taking care of that business as quickly and quietly as possible and out of sight of guests and others.

> I once needed a limousine for just a 1 1/2 hour run on a late Saturday afternoon that would be completed no later than 5:45 PM. The company quoted me a three hour minimum, which was fine. However, when they told me the wedding day was also a popular prom date and they'd have to leave promptly I told them that would be no problem but that my client shouldn't have to pay for three hours if they were only going to be able to have two hours which would result in their being paid twice for the same hour by two different clients. That was hardly fair to my client. They wouldn't negotiate on that and as a result lost my business that day and, more importantly, forever as I will never use that company again.

A well maintained vehicle or fleet is imperative. Both the inside and outside of your cars must be spotless and the outside free of dents or scrapes with no advertising or slogans. Cleaning the vehicle between clients or even between portions of the same run is important, and each car should be equipped with the tools to do that and your driver made aware that it's part of his job. No one wants to get into a car that looks less than fresh with remnants of a prior wedding, such as flower petals or used cocktail napkins or glasses on the floor, and time simply must be made to take care of that. It's not the client's fault that you have booked your gigs back to back and they should never even know that you are running so tight.

If you promise a bar or other beverages to the clients you must have it complete and exactly as promised with plenty of ice, cocktail napkins and decent, if not attractive, barware. I once heard an excuse that there was no Champagne left for a client because the prior client had drunk two bottles. How ridiculous. It's up to the driver to either dole out the Champagne properly, carry enough for all eventualities, or to replenish the supply between runs, even if that means stopping at a convenience store to do so. Again, it's not the client's fault if your driver is a poor manager.

Because there are many horror stories connected with limousine companies and drivers, the industry has a less than perfect reputation. Thus, any company with high standards and good business practices has a better than average chance of being successful and the conscientious owner will very likely quickly become known for dependability and professionalism. As with any business, going the extra mile for the client will pay off well.

Gratuities of 10 to 20% are customarily included in the price quoted for limousine service and that should be clearly stated in the contract. It must be made clear so the client understands that they do not have to tip anything extra unless they were ecstatic with the service. Or, if the gratuity is not included, the client must be made aware that it is customary to tip the driver. Because limousine service is not the norm in most people's lives and they have little experience with it, it is part of the booking agent's job to assist them in being comfortable with it so the day of the wedding is pleasant for them as well as for the driver.

Driver's attire is very important. The image of a liveried driver with a formal manner is probably most often conjured up when the word "limousine" is mentioned. Clients should be given the experience they expect by having your drivers clad in a dark suit and tie and even a traditional chauffeur's hat if the company wishes to portray that formal an image. A red carpet kept in the trunk to roll out for the passengers as they get in and out is a nice touch that gives a little more luxury to the ride and can be offered as a free option.

Your drivers should be trained to assist people in and out of the vehicles by offering a hand or taking packages or other items the riders are trying to handle. They should be willing to load wedding gifts or flowers or the like into the trunk or assist in other ways. I once ran into a limo driver who stood and watched several people moving wedding gifts into the trunk of the limo and when asked to help, said it wasn't his job to do that. I guess he figured he was hired to be a driver and that was all. That's what wrong with giving tips in advance.

Top limousine drivers make sure they have all the passengers they are to take before they drive away. Insist that your drivers check with the point person or have a list of their passengers to avoid leaving anyone behind. Especially at weddings, passengers can be distracted and not quite sure what is expected of them so the driver should assist as much as possible with that.

Buses, shuttles, and mini buses might be utilized to transport wedding guests from one location to another. Following a pre-determined route is important. Insist that your drivers check with the point person before deviating from the route at the request of a guest as such a deviation could throw off the entire schedule. In scheduling shuttle service it is important to consider how long each round trip will take especially if there are several destinations or stops. A ten minute ride from one point to another point becomes at least a 25 to 30 minute ride when the loading and unloading of passengers and travel both ways is factored in. Having more vehicles will alleviate long waits and more efficiently move the wedding guests in a timely manner.

Horses and carriages

There is something very romantic about having a horse drawn carriage transport a bride and groom on their wedding day. A carriage can be drawn by a single horse or team of horses and can be very simple or quite ornate, a la Cinderella. No matter which, all of the above information relating to limousines is applicable with additional requirements as discussed below.

As the carriage provider, you must make absolutely sure, through the wedding planner or your own research, that a horse and carriage will be allowed to traverse the route you will need to take. For example, back streets may need to be taken instead of a state highway or busy street that cannot accommodate as slow a vehicle as the carriage. Besides slowing traffic it can be dangerous to all concerned. If a permit is required by the local government it is your responsibility to obtain it or make certain the client or planner has obtained it. If safety equipment such as a flag or caution sign posted on the rear of the slow moving vehicle is required, again, as the carriage operator, it is your responsibility to make sure it is posted.

Naturally, the care and cleanup of the animal is your operator's responsibility. It is imperative that the animal be treated with the utmost kindness and consideration and not be overworked in the heat or expected to go long stretches without proper food and water. There is no such thing as minor mistreatment of an animal - all mistreatment is major and must absolutely be avoided.

A shovel and bag to dispose of waste should be included in the standard equipment.

Musicians for the Ceremony

Most often a different music group performs for the wedding ceremony and the reception. Often the ceremony music is classical or traditional. If the ceremony is in a church or other house of worship there might be an organist or other musical director whose services are offered and preferred by the site over an outside musician or group.

However, if you as outside musicians are allowed to play in the house of worship, whether solo or as part of a group, you must be very careful to abide by the rules and, particularly if you are not of the same faith, observe the customs or at least respect them as much as possible.

Some religious groups have strict rules about the kind of music allowed. For example, certain Catholic churches will not allow the familiar "Bridal Chorus" by Wagner or the "Wedding March" by Mendelssohn as these are not considered sacred music but show tunes, as they are from operas, which is in actuality musical theatre. No matter where the ceremony takes place many Jews will not have music written by certain composers played at their weddings because of those composers' anti-Semitic beliefs.

If you have never played at a particular location, check it out in advance - in person if at all possible or by phone with the wedding planner or officiant of the house of worship - both to become familiar with where your group will be placed and how to load your equipment in and out with the minimum of disruption. Many places have strict rules about parking vehicles and storing music cases and other equipment. Naturally, all such equipment should be out of sight of guests during the ceremony. It is important to arrive on time and be set up and ready to play at the appointed hour. A musician rushing in at the last minute is very unprofessional and will not be able to discuss cues and last minute changes to the ceremony that might necessitate adjustments.

Whether in a church, temple, hotel, or other wedding venue, a ceremony gig usually begins about a half an hour prior to the designated ceremony time with a half hour to an hour allowed for the ceremony. Many musicians have a two hour minimum and will continue to play for the cocktail or social hour prior to the meal. If the timing is lagging behind because of poor time management on the part of the wedding coordinator (horrors – she's in the wrong business!) or the wedding party and the time is up, the music can either be extended or your musicians can leave as planned.

Be sure to discuss the possibility of extending with the couple in advance of the wedding day so they know what to do if this issue arises. See "Extending Time" under "Bands" for a discussion of how this can be handled.

If a group being sent to perform for the ceremony does not normally play together it is very important that they rehearse the designated pieces of music in advance. I have seen too many pick up groups assemble at the ceremony site, set up their equipment then proceed to rehearse the designated ceremony songs as the guests are being seated This is very unprofessional and is a dead giveaway that they are not really a group. Upon closer examination they often have a ragtag look with different types of music stands in varying degrees of maintenance.

I once had a maid of honor who was attired in a very light dress and the leader of the classical group (hired by the bride and not one of my recommendations, I might point out) gave his group the signal for the "Bridal Chorus" as she appeared because he was not paying attention to my cues and just assumed she was the bride. When I began waving from the sidelines he caught on but it sounded terrible to change the music back for the maid of honor's entrance and then back again for the bride and took away some of the drama of the bride's entrance.

Top ceremony musicians take it upon themselves to check in with the wedding coordinator, or whoever is in charge of getting the bride down the aisle, to go over the music and cues as soon as they arrive. It's important that you know how many are in the processional and how long the path is so they know how many times you might have to play a song to get them all to the front. A flawless performance is important.

Since the music is very often traditional and thus familiar to the congregation they are likely to know when mistakes are made.

Because so many weddings take place out of doors it is important that you request an umbrella from the venue in advance or supply one yourself to protect your musicians and their instruments from the sun. The same is true for any chairs required. Some venues have arm chairs for the wedding guests and do not understand that a stringed instrument cannot easily be played in a chair with arms.

Microphones and sound systems must also be requested in advance and checked by your musicians immediately upon arrival. Some groups bring their own sound system and merely rely on the venue to supply the power source. In this case, the power must be checked at the beginning of the set up. There is no excuse to delay a wedding ceremony because the power isn't working properly.

You must keep your music stands and other equipment in good condition and your set up free of clutter. Piles of music books and empty cases make for a junky look, and all of that must be stowed neatly and out of sight. In outdoor performances that are subject to wind, clips must be used to hold the music down.

Attire for classical musicians is traditionally concert black with men in formal attire and women in conservative long gowns. The uniformity of all black gives a nice background for the beauty of the instruments as well as setting a more formal tone.

If you have to relocate after the ceremony to play during the cocktail hour always have two sets of chairs set up in advance so your group only has to pick up their instrument, music stand and other equipment and walk to the new location. Wasting your client's paid time by too much fussing around is unprofessional.

Officiants

There are many kinds of officiants for wedding ceremonies, including ministers either from a church or non-denominational, priests, rabbis, judges and more, but the common goal of their job is simply to perform the ceremony that unites the bride and groom in marriage. Actually, the officiant, the couple, the marriage license and possibly two witnesses to sign the license are the only necessary elements of the wedding. The rest is fluff. Expensive fluff to be sure, but fluff nonetheless.

In some religious orders the marriage ceremony is a sacrament and is to be taken very seriously while in other religions or in non-religious ceremonies there is less formality. It is up to you as the officiant to impart the parameters of the ceremony to the couple and the wedding party, though most couples who are active in a religion know what to expect from it. However, because of the high occurrence of interfaith weddings these days, one of the couple may not be familiar with what is required.

Many officiants do not attend the wedding rehearsal and that is fine. However, it is important that you go over the ceremony with the couple during one of their pre-wedding meetings and also have a conversation with the coordinator to give her information that will allow her to instruct the wedding party properly. (Note to coordinators: it is your job to contact the officiant to obtain all the information you need to properly direct the rehearsal and to ascertain in advance if any props are necessary which you, the venue or the couple are responsible for providing. Examples would be a table, a riser, a microphone, wine and/or glasses for a wine ceremony.)

If you are an officiant that does attend the rehearsal and there is a wedding coordinator, you must keep in mind that she is overseeing the whole wedding day and is very much tuned in to what is happening. The two of you should think of your relationship as a partnership, with the goal of making the bride and groom's day a very happy one. Even if you direct the entire rehearsal, it is considerate of you to introduce the wedding coordinator and state her title. If you can allow her to have a few moments to speak to the wedding party at the end of the rehearsal that would be very polite as the rehearsal is most likely the first time she will have met most, if not all, of the bridesmaids and groomsmen and many other family members. It will contribute to the smoothness of the wedding day for all of them to be aware of her and what she is there to do.

Please see the section above entitled "Churches / Ceremony Sites" above.

An officiant has the same requirements of professionalism as any other vendor, which include punctuality, being a team player, being organized and returning phone calls and following up with the clients. As a representative of God you might even be held to a higher standard because of that connection and expectation of living in His shadow.

A note on discussions you have with the bride and groom in the pre-wedding meetings: Brides and grooms tend to be put-off by discussions or questionnaires that include references to sex. Many times, I have heard from them and other wedding planners that they are generally not comfortable talking about this either if you have a church relationship with them or are hired strictly for the wedding ceremony. Even if you are a licensed counselor, I strongly suggest you tread very lightly in this area - if you tread at all. It can be a deal breaker.

Photographers

A photographer is an integral part of most weddings and is often one of the first vendors to be hired during the wedding planning process. Most brides and grooms have definite ideas of the type of photography they like, whether if be traditional (more posed), candid, which is sometimes called photojournalism in today's parlance, color, black and white, sepia or a combination of those.

Photography is often a large part of the wedding budget because the captured memories are very important to the couple and the day's events will never take place again. Thus, it is important that the photographer produce high quality photos of every major activity of the wedding and a great many minor ones as well. The bridal couple will most likely be involved in all the major events of the day but will be delighted to see photos of some of the minor things that happened on the other side of the room or before they were together for the ceremony.

Discuss in advance with the bride and groom exactly what they expect and what you can give them. Promise only what you can actually deliver. Obtain a list in advance of the wedding day of the "must-have" group shots and ask them to designate a family member from each side who can assist you in rounding up those subjects or you risk wasting time looking for them or miss them altogether, which is something many brides and grooms will not forgive.

Top wedding photographers have a second shooter with them or at least an assistant to carry equipment and change lenses, etc. Some will have two second shooters and an assistant but naturally the cost of their services is going to be higher.

The best wedding photographers are un-intrusive, low key and highly professional in manner and appearance. Keep in mind that you and the videographer will be after the same shots and, whether you've met one another before the wedding day or not, you are part of the same team. Thus you must be aware of the other's needs and respect them.

As a top wedding photographer you will cooperate with the producer of the timeline and work within it as much as possible, making sure you do not remove the bride or the couple from their guests for protracted periods of time. One of the biggest complaints from guests is that photos took so long that the cocktail hour is prolonged to such a length that it becomes boring. This also causes the guests to become overly inebriated and can increase the cost of the bar tab considerably.

The whole point of the wedding day is for the bridal couple to pledge their vows before the people most important to them and then to celebrate the happy occasion with them at the reception. They should be allowed to spend as much time with their family and friends as possible rather than being taken away for endless portraits just so you have more poses to sell them.

Speaking of selling, the top wedding photographers do not base their income on upselling the bride and groom albums and photos after the wedding. Instead they base their fee on their shooting time and get paid for that and their talent. They might include certain albums or prints in their package prices, but that is known up front. Unscrupulous photographers often advertise a very low price "wedding package" with the intention of upselling to increase their bottom line. Less experienced wedding couples are enticed by the low price and perceive it as a bargain only to be pressured or shamed into buying more than they might have intended or could afford.

To become a top wedding photographer you will have honed your craft so you are quick at getting the best shots and photograph what is happening, not what you want to happen by staging the shots. The term "photojournalism" is bandied about today so much that is has almost become a cliché, and many photographers and brides have no idea what it really is. True photojournalism is the telling of a news story by use of photos rather than words and most often uses raw, un-retouched photos to capture of an event. Candid shots are actually what most wedding "photojournalism" really is, in that the photo subjects are being captured while acting spontaneously and naturally rather than being posed. They may not even be aware that their photo is being taken.

> One couple told me about the $1500 package they bought that turned into a $5000 package after all was said and done. The photographer was only average and if, going in, they had known they'd be spending that much, they would have just hired the $5000 photographer with the better talent and reputation.

Sometimes a bride will emphatically state that she wants no posed shots, but then ask for group photos of her family. It's ridiculous to think that you could get a candid shot of a sizeable family group who just happened to be together and facing the camera when the photographer was passing by. In this case you must ferret out what she is really asking for. Is it no posed shots for the activities she and the groom will participate in? Is it that she wants some good candid shots along with the family portraits? Or does she just want to avoid the stiff look of old-fashioned wedding photography with the lines of attendants saying "cheese" for the camera?

It's important for you to get the proofs to the bride and groom in a timely manner and, as soon as the couple has decided on their favorite shots, work with them to get any albums they order into production and finished. Many couples are shocked at the number of months it takes to get their finished album but, of course, they are responsible for the delay if they failed to select and return the proofs timely. There are so many ways of getting proofs to the bride and groom now with the advent of online proofing services. Gone are the days when the one set of proofs had to be shipped around the country so every key family member could mark his or her favorites before passing them to the next person.

> I once sat in on a meeting between and bride and a young photographer who was very excited about his digital camera and the ability he had to edit the photos so easily via his laptop. He showed how he added a sunset to a photo that was shot digitally against a plain white wall. While that is a technical feat, the bride saw it as tinkering with the photos and didn't want a photographer who was making images that were not really what he saw or what actually happened.

With the advent of digital cameras some photographers are using that method exclusively and eschewing film to shoot weddings. Other photographers use a combination of digital and film and still others are using only film believing that digital has yet to be perfected to the point that they will trust a wedding to it. Which method you chose is a matter of preference and a decision between you and your clients.

Some photographers wrongly propound the notion they are entitled to eat in the reception room with the guests and expect a place setting at a guest table. The excuse they give is that they'll miss some shots while they are out of the room. If they are out of the room having a quick meal during the guests' meal it's highly unlikely that the bride wants to be photographed while she is chewing anyway.

At a well-timed reception the vendor breaks are taken during the guests' meal and those breaks are no longer than 20 minutes, and often less, allowing just enough time to refresh before the next phase of the reception. If you are very concerned about it, simply have your second shooter stay in the room to catch such shots while you have a quick bite and vice versa. Or you can eat before you come to the wedding and skip the vendor meal altogether. After all, providing a meal for vendors is a favor the bride is doing and while I advocate having them, if it becomes an issue with how you do your job, it should be handled accordingly. Top wedding photographers do not expect to be treated as a guest. Please read the section above entitled "Behavior, Manners and Etiquette".

Decide in advance with your clients how you will handle overtime charges if you are required to stay longer than contracted should the wedding activities run overtime. Most photographers are willing to stay an extra 15 or even 30 minutes outside the contracted time just to finish up with any major activities they need to catch. However, when it becomes more than a half hour they will begin to add an overtime charge. Will you bill the client later for it or do you expect to be paid right on the spot? Being paid on the spot can be a little awkward for the client who then has to fish around in their pocket or handbag to find some cash or a check. Since most brides don't carry such items in their wedding handbag it becomes a distraction that can interfere with the mood of the reception. Because of this, and also because you have a product to be delivered after the fact, any overtime charge should just be added to the final total as long as you have authorization for it.

One huge marketing opportunity that you can take advantage of is sending photos to other vendors showing those vendors' work at a wedding you photographed. This has a triple purpose of delighting the vendor with a professional photo they can use in their portfolio, having your work be seen by brides in other people's portfolios (don't forget to identify the work as yours by signing the photo or laminating it with your company name) and giving you

Two opposite attitudes that I have encountered are the well known photographer who very generously gives out photos to everyone even remotely connected with the wedding, thus having her work seen by brides at almost every wedding vendor they visit from the florist to the cake baker to the caterer, versus another photographer, whose work is equally good, but complains that she sees no reason why she has to give photos free to other vendors saying she's the only vendor expected to do that. It's clear who "gets it" here and who doesn't. In fact, the latter photographer is no longer doing weddings after trying to break in to the market and giving up after a couple of years.

a reputation for being generous and sharing with others and being part of the team. The latter will come about especially if you get these photos out very quickly after a spectacular wedding and into the portfolios of your fellow vendors.

In fact, there are several outstanding, well known photographers whom I do not refer simply because they never supply me with photos of weddings we've done together, even when I offer to pay for them. I reason that if I had to build my portfolio based on their cooperation it would be very slim indeed. Because my portfolio is such an important marketing tool I always refer the talented photographers that get photos to me timely.

Rental Companies

There are many weddings in which no outside rentals are utilized, some with just an item or two and others with truck loads of things from tables to silverware. Whichever category a wedding falls into, the two most important considerations a client will expect are promptness of delivery and pickup and quality and maintenance of the rental items. The breadth of the offerings is another huge consideration, along with professionalism of the staff from the office personnel to the truck drivers and delivery men.

Top rental companies are open to adding items to their inventory and might even custom-make things that will enhance their inventory. For example, long, narrow and square dining tables have become popular for weddings and such an item will likely be rented over and over, giving your company an edge.

Some rental companies specialize in certain items such as fine china, unusual and sumptuous linens, tents of all shapes and sizes, or residential furniture groupings. Others will carry a range of basic rentals with an emphasis on certain things that their clients have come to expect, such as silver tabletop décor (e.g. chargers, vases, epergnes, or cake stands) or a wide range of chairs (e.g. Chiavari chairs in a myriad of colors, brushed aluminum or modern style). Specialization can be a very good thing but it's most important that prospective clients be aware of what you have so you can rent it out often.

A well appointed showroom where planners and caterers can bring clients to view your set up is a must. The room must be well lighted and free of clutter and should have display tables where your products such as linens, dishes and chairs can be tried out. Because many people are visual this provides an opportunity for them to see your rentals at their best.

Providing an empty table where clients can put together their own ideas with your inventory and having one of your staff members available to assist such clients is an important marketing tool. Orders can be written or refined at this time and new products can be shown that might be of interest to the client.

Allowing planners and caterers to take out some samples on memo for a day or so to show their clients without incurring a rental charge is another way to show your rental inventory. The easier you make it for those vendors the better your sales will ultimately be. Some rental companies even let their best customers have a small permanent display in their own place of business because they know this adds to their sales as well.

A well maintained and up-to-date website is as important for a rental company as for any other wedding business – maybe even more so. A wedding planner or caterer might be familiar with certain of the items you carry but might want to show it to their client. Many brides live away from the area where they are being married and plan from a distance, so being able to refer them to your website to use as a catalog is extremely helpful. Make sure the photos you post are clear and show accurately the variety of colors you're carrying. Be sure to describe the product including size and unusual characteristics. When you have new rental inventory to market letting the caterers and planners know about it via the website is a great marketing tool. A postcard can be sent to your mailing list three or four times a year letting your clients know about your new additions. Besides keeping your company name in front of them it will also cause them to visit your website more frequently.

Outstanding customer service with a knowledgeable and professional staff will place your rental company in the top echelon. If you have competitive prices it will further your reputation, but the former two qualities will outweigh the latter one. Cheap prices alone will not sustain your business over the long haul, especially if you wish to be a top rental company.

It is very common in the rental industry to offer a 10% discount to bona fide wedding professionals. Some rental companies will quote the full retail price in their catalog then give the discount to the wedding professional by means of a commission check after the event is completed. Others will show such discount on the invoice of the wedding professional and expect them to mark up the item to retail and bill their client accordingly. While the former method entails more bookkeeping for the rental company in that they might have to issue 1099 forms at the end of the year, many wedding professionals prefer that to having to book the rentals in their company name then invoicing their client for the difference so they can take the markup. You will have to determine how your company is going to treat each of your clients – will it be all the same way or according to their individual preference?

Make clear in advance who is responsible for shortages, damage or breakage. Generally it is the person whose name is on your order whether that is the bride and groom, the planner or the caterer. Caterers or planners will often pass that cost on to their clients and should advise them in advance of this responsibility so there are no surprises when the event is over. You might consider offering some optional low cost insurance to all customers that will build a fund to cover breakage, but that is a business decision to discuss with your accountant or lawyer.

Servers/Waiters

Service is an important part of every dining experience and can often make or break the guests' overall impression. If I had to make a choice (though I would prefer not to) I would take mediocre food and great service over the other way around. The best service is made up of a well trained staff in a plentiful number. Top wedding venues such as five star hotels assign one server to every fifteen guests; four star hotels server to guest ratio is about twenty guests while a staff that is stretched has to handle 25 or more guests each. Anything more than that is unfair to the guests and the staff alike.

Naturally the serving staff's efficiency is greatly influenced by the kitchen and how they are turning out the food, but for now we must assume they are doing their job as expected. (However, if they are not, an overhaul in that end of the establishment could be in order but that is beyond the scope of this book.)

As top service staff, you must be trained to anticipate your guests' needs and to react politely to their requests. You must pleasantly acknowledge a guest or smile while performing your duties while in the public view. If you are not able to do this consistently you are probably in the wrong business and should do all concerned a favor and find another career.

Small details, such as refolding a guest's napkin when they get up, refilling water glasses before they are empty, asking before pouring more wine, and presenting all plates so the entrée is placed in the same direction are the details that make a memorable dining experience.

All servers should be briefed on the contents of the food and its preparation. If asked you must be able to answer simple questions posed by a diner. For example, whether the soup is made with meat stock is a very important question to a vegetarian. If the dish contains peanuts or mushrooms or another ingredient that can cause a violent or even fatal allergic reaction in certain people it must be answered accurately. Too much can be at stake for you to just make up an answer out of laziness. More complex questions must be taken to the chef or banquet captain for an answer which is then conveyed quickly to the inquiring guest.

As part of the serving staff you should do just that – serve. You should not engage in extended conversations with guests, wedding vendors or, worse yet, your own colleagues. Guests don't generally care to hear about their server's personal life. When not actually serving and clearing, you and your fellow servers should stand on the sidelines to be ready to assist any guests, whether at your assigned table or not, with any needs they have.

Your attire must be clean and neat and fit properly. Long hair must be tied back or up and fingernails must be short and clean and free of colored nail polish. Do not wear perfume or fragrance, and choose unscented deodorant - but be sure you wear the latter! White glove service is used in finer establishments and each server must be provided with several sets of white gloves which are always pristine or the whole image goes out the window.

Knowing and using good manners is essential as you interact with guests. As a server you will encounter people from all walks of life. All must be treated politely and kindly and referred to as Sir or Ma'am or Miss. It is important that your demeanor not become overly formal and so stiff or impersonal that it smacks of rudeness or indifference.

Tuxedo Rental Companies

Many men are not used to wearing formal dress and rely on a rental company to provide them with advice on the proper attire for their wedding. Great service, well maintained rental clothing, and education are all important elements of a good formalwear rental company. Add to that, convenient, well decorated and well maintained locations, long hours of operation, a wide variety of choices, and an expert staff and you have a top company.

One of the major recurring complaints I hear from the men's wedding party is that elements of their rental attire are missing when they are ready to dress, or that something is egregiously the wrong size. Having each customer try on his garments including shirt and shoes before leaving the store is obviously the most fool-proof way to avoid this. However, since many men in a wedding party are not even in town until the day or evening before the wedding, and their formalwear is ordered via telephone or over the internet from a set of body measurements, which may or may not be accurate, this becomes problematical.

A formalwear company that offers, for an upcharge, the service of delivering all the men's rented attire directly to their hotel at a convenient time before the wedding can get a reputation for being highly service oriented. Being prepared to return to quickly replace any improperly fitted or missing items, or even bringing a few back up items in varying sizes is an important part of that service. As an additional service, you can also arrange to return the next day to pick up all attire after the wedding as well.

While pinning on boutonnieres at one wedding two groomsmen were complaining that their rental clothes didn't fit properly – one set was too short and the other too long, the shoes were too big or too small. It turned out they had mixed them up and were actually wearing each other's clothes. It was a rather amusing sight watching them hustle off to trade clothes and they came back looking and feeling much better.

Having a member of your staff or a courier on call to rapidly replace any missing or ill fitting items (whether it's your company's fault or not) within a short period of time can often save the day for the wedding party and give your company a great reputation among wedding vendors and clients alike. Many members of a wedding party are going to be a groom someday themselves and their perception of your company as a service-oriented, well-run company is another form of advertising for you. These are just more forms of possible referral business.

Sometimes the proper sizes are sent but the men mix them up, so if you get a call about things not fitting the first thing you might ask is whether they actually have on the clothing that was sent for them.

Many clients have no idea that a black tuxedo is actually evening wear and incorrect before six in the evening. If they are having a day wedding, they might chose to break the rule and wear a tuxedo anyway. However, it is your company's job to inform them of this and show them the proper daytime attire. It is also your responsibility to advise the groom and his attendants the proper way to wear certain pieces of attire. If a bow tie is not pre-tied make certain someone in the wedding party is capable of tying that kind of tie - it's not just tying a bow like one uses for shoelaces. Make sure they know how to place a pocket square and studs as well. Even the simplest things can be a puzzle for someone not used to wearing them.

The best man is often the person designated to return the tuxedos after the wedding so you must make sure he understands the time and place of drop off. Since that could likely be on a Sunday top rental companies have provisions for such even if the store isn't open.

Valets

Valet service is a luxury item for some weddings and a necessity for others. Any off-premise event in a location that has no convenient parking must offer it and, even if there is convenient self-parking, it's a gracious way to greet arriving guests.

The top valet companies supply appropriately attired parking attendants who are cordial to arriving guests and drive their cars carefully. They are painstakingly aware of security and keep the car keys locked and out of reach of passersby, especially if the valet stand is not going to be attended at all times. Do not change radio stations or seat adjustments in guests' automobiles and do not even think of picking up small change off the dashboard or taking anything such as sunglasses or pens from a car. That is stealing and no top notch company has employees who steal.

Offering options for the parking attendants' attire such as Hawaiian shirts and Bermuda shorts for an island themed event, black slacks, white shirts and bow ties for a more formal event or khakis and white polo shirts for a casual day event is a nice addition to your service. Some of the best valet companies will not allow their employees to wear earrings or body piercings, have visible tattoos or to have facial hair or long hair, even if tied back.

If there is rain or inclement weather expected and there is no covering over the arrival area, top valet companies supply large golf umbrellas under which guests are escorted to the front door and/or back to their cars. It's an extra touch but much appreciated by the host and guest alike.

Tips at a private event are generally included in the fee charged to the host and the guests are not expected to further tip the valets. However, if a guest offers, some companies allow their valets to accept it with gracious thanks.

Ironclad Rule #24: **<u>Never</u> place any kind of tip jar or receptacle at a private function.**

Because many valets are young people (who else can run like that all evening?) it is important that they be supervised by a more mature and responsible company employee. It goes without saying that the best valet services are highly insured with the most reliable insurance company and carry all necessary coverage including Comprehensive Liability and Garage Keepers Legal Liability as well as Worker's Compensation. All employees are obviously expected to be experienced licensed drivers who are responsible drivers with no accident record and will not even think of joy riding even if the most primo Ferrari arrives to be parked.

Videographers

Wedding videography can be as simple as a single unmanned camera being placed stationary during the reception to a full multi-camera production that includes recording the entire setup and preparation of the wedding site all the way to the departure of the bride and groom. While these two examples are extremes and most wedding videos fall somewhere in the middle, some brides and grooms are concerned that a videographer will be intrusive and take away from their and their guests' enjoyment of the wedding day.

Some of the most egregious behavior of wedding videographers I have ever witnessed was the use of not one but two rolling tripods whose bases were at least two feet in diameter and which were wheeled around the room in what seemed like constant pursuit of the wedding couple. Coupled with the bright lights and an equally intrusive duo of photographers these very unprofessional vendors actually prevented the parents and other family and friends of the bridal couple from seeing activities such as the cake cutting and bouquet toss, as they were lined up like paparazzi whenever the MC invited the guests' to watch such activities. These vendors were hired by the bride and groom before they hired me and I added them to my personal "do not refer" list immediately.

Possibly the biggest concern is having a bright light shining during filming followed by the fear that the videographer will thrust a microphone in their guest's face for comments. So as a top videographer you should be very aware of these concerns and avoid them at all costs.

The top wedding videographers, just as the top wedding photographers, are there to document what is naturally happening at the wedding and reception, not to make things happen for the camera by posing the subjects or setting up situations. With today's compact equipment and fast film it is virtually unnecessary for a videographer to have huge cameras and bright lights and boom microphones.

If you plan to incorporate guest interviews into the finished product make sure the bride and groom agree to your approaching guests for this purpose. Some couples nix it altogether, some say do it if the guests volunteer to be videoed, and others want you to actively solicit interviews. Either way, you must be gracious as you interact with the guests and be mindful of your position as an observer and documenter and not become too familiar or informal with the guests

The photographer and videographer must work as a team, even if they are meeting for the very first time at the wedding. One of the worst things you can do is to place yourselves so you are constantly in each other's shots. This also holds true for the coordinator and other vendors who should be aware of where they are in relation to the photos being taken.

You should conduct yourself as professionally as any other vendor during all phases of the job by wearing the appropriate attire for the occasion and observing the practices as described above in the section entitled "Behavior, Manners and Etiquette". Also please refer to the above section on "Photography".

Editing is an extremely important component of an outstanding product and one that requires technical skill as well as artistry. The best footage in the world can be ruined if not well edited and, on the other side of the coin, brilliant editing might make average footage look better than it is. Of course, having great footage and great editing will get you a dynamite product.

Titles and other graphics must be carefully incorporated and chosen to enhance the finished product rather than dominate it. The same consideration must be given to the background music. Stay on top of the trends in the video industry so you can be aware of what is current. Titles, colors and graphics can date your work and too much of it can be distracting to the viewer.

Add-ons you can offer are photo montages of the couple growing up or even mini movies of how their relationship developed after they met that can be shown at the rehearsal dinner or reception (I had one couple show theirs at the ceremony!). If you undertake to provide the technical aspect of the presentation, be sure you have arranged in advance for the screen, extension cords and other paraphernalia you will need. The presentation must be carried out quickly and unobtrusively with the minimum of disruption.

Web casting or live streaming of weddings is a recent addition to the videographer's repertoire so you might look into offering that. It will probably become wide spread quickly.

Barbara Wallace

Appendices

A. Service Questionnaire
B. Protocol for Assistants
C. Priority Ranking of Wedding Elements by Bride and Groom

Appendix A

SERVICE QUESTIONNAIRE

Name_____

Wedding Date_____

Services provided_____

In an ongoing effort to make sure I help my clients have a wonderful wedding, I would like to ask you to take a few moments to answer the following questions. Please be as straightforward and detailed as you like.

What part of my service was <u>most</u> important to you?

_____

_____

What part of my service was <u>least</u> important to you?

_____

_____

Is there anything I could have done to better serve you?

_____

_____

Was the service worth what you paid?

_____ Why?_____

_____

Barbara Wallace

Did I do what I said I was going to do or what you expected me to do?

_____

_____

How would you rate the quality of my service?

_____

_____

Would you recommend me to another bride?

_____

_____

_____

Please rate the vendors that I referred to you.

_____

_____

_____

Additional Comments

_____

_____

Thank you for your time

Appendix B

PROTOCOL FOR ASSISTANTS, INTERNS AND NOVICES

Giving the highest level of service to clients is of utmost importance. They should have an experience that is as close to perfect as possible so they come away with beautiful memories of their wedding day. Our attention to detail will enhance their experience and that of their guests. Therefore I ask that you practice the following when you are working at one of my weddings. Thank you for being part of a winning team.

1. Please dress in the prescribed business attire. My preference is a conservative dark business suit (either skirt or pants) and a cream or white shell. Suit jacket must have pockets for your copy of the timeline and a belt or waistband to hang the walkie-talkie on. We will discuss this in advance. Please wear comfortable closed-toe shoes (no spikes, sandals or slides) and nylons. I suggest you bring a change to flat heels. You'll be happier after a few hours. No visible tattoos or body piercings (except one earring per ear). Jewelry is to be conservative i.e. no multiple rings or dangling earrings. Makeup and hair are to be neat and in a conservative style i.e. no unusual colors of hair, nail polish, lipstick or eye shadow.

2. Please review the timeline in advance to become familiar with what you are expected to do. Discuss in advance anything that is not clear.

3. Please arrive at the time you are expected. Please check with me before departing to make sure all work is finished.

4. Please become familiar with the walkie-talkie system (if used) and put it on immediately upon arrival and keeping it on as long as necessary

5. Please keep paperwork and personal belongings out of sight of guests and help see that no other clutter is lying around. Guests should not see the timeline and things that pertain to "behind the scenes". This also applies to all vendors whose things are to be kept out of sight of guests as much as possible. Under the gift or cake tables is usually a good place to stash things. It's best not to bring a purse or backpack along. We have

limited space to store things and there is always a slight chance that things can be stolen.

6. Please do not bring or distribute your business cards or mention your own business. If anyone asks for a card, please have some of mine handy to give to them.

7. Regarding questions from guests, vendors or venue staff, please use your best judgment and knowledge in answering them but if you cannot easily answer, please find someone who can as soon as possible then follow up with the answer to the person who posed the question.

8. Please be gracious and polite at all times even if it means biting your tongue sometimes. Your assistance in keeping the atmosphere pleasant is much appreciated.

9. Please do not take photos without permission and do not expect to use photos from events other than your own in your portfolio

10. Please do not eat or drink in front of guests at any time. We are hired help, not guests and hors d'oeuvres and other food and beverages are not for us. Drinking of alcoholic beverages at any time is expressly forbidden. Vendor meals will be eaten during our break, which will be taken at a reasonable and convenient time during the course of the reception.

11. Please carry and use a few breath mints (no gum)

12. Please do not initiate more than polite conversation with guests unless it pertains to the flow of the event – we are here to work, not visit.

13. Please become familiar with the location of the restrooms and other places to which guests might need to be directed.

Appendix C

BARBARA WALLACE WEDDINGS
BRIDE AND GROOM'S PRIORITY LIST
PLEASE RANK EACH ITEM IN ORDER OF IMPORTANCE
1 = very important; 2 = moderately important; 3= not important

Names_____

Wedding Element	Bride's Rank	Groom's Rank	Compromise
1. Ceremony Location			
2. Reception Location			
3. Ceremony Décor			
4. Reception Décor			
5. Flowers			
6. Invitations/Stationery			
7. Size of Guest List			
8. Food			
9. Beverage			
10. Service Staff/Style			
11. Bride/Groom Attire			
12. Attendant's Attire			
13. Size of Bridal Party			
14. Photography			

Barbara Wallace

15. Videography

16. Wedding Cake

17. Music/Entertainment at reception

18. Music at Ceremony

19. Traditions

20. Favors/Souvenirs

21. Rehearsal Dinner

Trade Organizations

ADJA - American Disk Jockey Association
2000 Corporate Dr., #408, Ladera Ranch, CA. 92694
888 723-5776
www.adja.com

AWPI- Association for Wedding Professionals, Inc.
2740 Arden Way, Suite 100, Sacramento, CA. 95825
800 242-4461
www.afwpi.com

ABC – Association of Bridal Consultants
56 Danbury Road, Suite 11, New Milford, CT. 06776
860 355-0464
www.bridalassn.com

ISES - International Special Events Society
401 N. Michigan Avenue, Chicago, IL. 60611-4267
800 688-4737
www.ises.com

JWI - June Weddings, Inc.
584 Castro Street, #452, San Francisco, CA 94114-2594
469 241-1480
www.junewedding.com

PPA- Professional Photographers of America, Inc
220 Peachtree St. NE, Suite 220, Atlanta, GA. 30303
800 786-6277
www.ppa.com

WEVA – Wedding and Event Videographers Association International
8499 S. Tamiami Trail, PMB 208, Sarasota, FL. 34238
941 923-5334
www.weva.com

Barbara Wallace

Suggested Reading

Dress For Success by John T. Molloy

Guerilla Marketing by Jay Conrad Levinson

Nichecraft by Dr. Lynda Falkenstein

Make a Name for Yourself by Robin Fisher Roffer

Dollars and Events *How To Succeed in the Special Events Business* by Dr. Joe Goldblatt, CSEP and Frank Supovitz

The International Dictionary of Event Management by Dr. Joe Goldblatt, CSEP and Kathleen S. Nelson, Editors

Behind the Scenes at Special Events by Lena Malouf

Special Events, Third Edition by Dr. Joe Goldblatt, CSEP

About the Author

Barbara Wallace is a highly regarded full service wedding planner located in Corona del Mar, California and winner of a 2001 Gala Award from Special Events Magazine. She was also nominated for a Gala Award in 2002. She is widely recognized as the premier wedding planner in Orange County (California). Barbara is a creative thinker who enjoys helping to customize a wedding to exactly fit the personalities of the bride and groom. She is referred by such respected wedding venues as the Ritz-Carlton Laguna Niguel; Montage Resort and Spa, Laguna Beach; Hyatt Regency Huntington Beach Resort and Spa; St. Regis Monarch Beach Resort and Spa; Hyatt Regency Irvine; and Four Seasons Newport Beach.

Barbara has traveled widely and has a deep interest in other cultures. She earned a BS in Fashion Design, Textiles and Merchandising from the University of Hawai'i (Manoa). She also holds a J.D. from Western State University.

Barbara, President and founder of Barbara Wallace Weddings, holds the designation Master Bridal Consultant (less than forty-five people in the world have earned this designation and Barbara is the only one in Orange County, California) from the Association of Bridal Consultants (ABC) and is a Distinguished Graduate of their program. She keeps abreast of the latest trends through continuing education, speaking engagements and attendance at ABC national and state conferences and local networking groups as well as The Special Event and various other trade events. She is the Co-director of the Association of Bridal Consultants, Orange County Local Networking Group. She is also a member of the International Special Events Society (ISES) and is working on obtaining the Certified Special Events Professional (CSEP) designation.

Order Form

To order additional copies of the Wedding Vendor Handbook, please visit Amazon.com or send a check or money order, along with a copy of this form, to:

Sage House Publishing
PO Box 84
Corona del Mar, CA 92625-0084

Per single copy: $21.95 + $5.95 shipping & handling = $27.90
5 or more copies (to same address): $19.95 + $3.95 = $23.90 per copy

Quantity	Price	Total

Sub-Total $_____

7.75% Sales Tax (CA only) $_____

Shipping & delivery $_____

Total $_____

Ship to:

Name: _____

Address: _____

City: _____ State: _____ Zip: _____

Order Form

To order additional copies of the Wedding Vendor Handbook, please visit www.sagehousepublishing.com or send a check or money order, along with a copy of this form, to:

Sage House Publishing
PO Box 84
Corona del Mar, CA 92625-0084

Per single copy: $21.95 + $5.95 shipping & handling = $27.90
5 or more copies (to same address): $19.95 + $3.95 = $23.90 per copy

Quantity	Price	Total

Sub-Total $_____

7.75% Sales Tax (CA only) $_____

Shipping & delivery $_____

Total $_____

Ship to:

Name: _____

Address: _____

City: _____ State: ____ Zip: _____

In case we need to contact you about this order:

Email:_____

Daytime phone number:_____